FREE Test Taking Tips DVD Offer

To help us better serve you, we have developed a Test Taking Tips DVD that we would like to give you for FREE. **This DVD covers world-class test taking tips that you can use to be even more successful when you are taking your test.**

All that we ask is that you email us your feedback about your study guide. Please let us know what you thought about it – whether that is good, bad or indifferent.

To get your **FREE Test Taking Tips DVD**, email freedvd@studyguideteam.com with "FREE DVD" in the subject line and the following information in the body of the email:

a. The title of your study guide.

b. Your product rating on a scale of 1-5, with 5 being the highest rating.

c. Your feedback about the study guide. What did you think of it?

d. Your full name and shipping address to send your free DVD.

If you have any questions or concerns, please don't hesitate to contact us at freedvd@studyguideteam.com.

Thanks again!

ACCUPLACER English Study Guide 2019-2020

ACCUPLACER Reading Comprehension, Sentence Skills, and Writing Test Prep & 2 Practice Tests

Test Prep Books

Table of Contents

Quick Overview

As you draw closer to taking your exam, effective preparation becomes more and more important. Thankfully, you have this study guide to help you get ready. Use this guide to help keep your studying on track and refer to it often.

This study guide contains several key sections that will help you be successful on your exam. The guide contains tips for what you should do the night before and the day of the test. Also included are test-taking tips. Knowing the right information is not always enough. Many well-prepared test takers struggle with exams. These tips will help equip you to accurately read, assess, and answer test questions.

A large part of the guide is devoted to showing you what content to expect on the exam and to helping you better understand that content. In this guide are practice test questions so that you can see how well you have grasped the content. Then, answer explanations are provided so that you can understand why you missed certain questions.

Don't try to cram the night before you take your exam. This is not a wise strategy for a few reasons. First, your retention of the information will be low. Your time would be better used by reviewing information you already know rather than trying to learn a lot of new information. Second, you will likely become stressed as you try to gain a large amount of knowledge in a short amount of time. Third, you will be depriving yourself of sleep. So be sure to go to bed at a reasonable time the night before. Being well-rested helps you focus and remain calm.

Be sure to eat a substantial breakfast the morning of the exam. If you are taking the exam in the afternoon, be sure to have a good lunch as well. Being hungry is distracting and can make it difficult to focus. You have hopefully spent lots of time preparing for the exam. Don't let an empty stomach get in the way of success!

When travelling to the testing center, leave earlier than needed. That way, you have a buffer in case you experience any delays. This will help you remain calm and will keep you from missing your appointment time at the testing center.

Be sure to pace yourself during the exam. Don't try to rush through the exam. There is no need to risk performing poorly on the exam just so you can leave the testing center early. Allow yourself to use all of the allotted time if needed.

Remain positive while taking the exam even if you feel like you are performing poorly. Thinking about the content you should have mastered will not help you perform better on the exam.

Once the exam is complete, take some time to relax. Even if you feel that you need to take the exam again, you will be well served by some down time before you begin studying again. It's often easier to convince yourself to study if you know that it will come with a reward!

Test-Taking Strategies

1. Predicting the Answer

When you feel confident in your preparation for a multiple-choice test, try predicting the answer before reading the answer choices. This is especially useful on questions that test objective factual knowledge. By predicting the answer before reading the available choices, you eliminate the possibility that you will be distracted or led astray by an incorrect answer choice. You will feel more confident in your selection if you read the question, predict the answer, and then find your prediction among the answer choices. After using this strategy, be sure to still read all of the answer choices carefully and completely. If you feel unprepared, you should not attempt to predict the answers. This would be a waste of time and an opportunity for your mind to wander in the wrong direction.

2. Reading the Whole Question

Too often, test takers scan a multiple-choice question, recognize a few familiar words, and immediately jump to the answer choices. Test authors are aware of this common impatience, and they will sometimes prey upon it. For instance, a test author might subtly turn the question into a negative, or he or she might redirect the focus of the question right at the end. The only way to avoid falling into these traps is to read the entirety of the question carefully before reading the answer choices.

3. Looking for Wrong Answers

Long and complicated multiple-choice questions can be intimidating. One way to simplify a difficult multiple-choice question is to eliminate all of the answer choices that are clearly wrong. In most sets of answers, there will be at least one selection that can be dismissed right away. If the test is administered on paper, the test taker could draw a line through it to indicate that it may be ignored; otherwise, the test taker will have to perform this operation mentally or on scratch paper. In either case, once the obviously incorrect answers have been eliminated, the remaining choices may be considered. Sometimes identifying the clearly wrong answers will give the test taker some information about the correct answer. For instance, if one of the remaining answer choices is a direct opposite of one of the eliminated answer choices, it may well be the correct answer. The opposite of obviously wrong is obviously right! Of course, this is not always the case. Some answers are obviously incorrect simply because they are irrelevant to the question being asked. Still, identifying and eliminating some incorrect answer choices is a good way to simplify a multiple-choice question.

4. Don't Overanalyze

Anxious test takers often overanalyze questions. When you are nervous, your brain will often run wild, causing you to make associations and discover clues that don't actually exist. If you feel that this may be a problem for you, do whatever you can to slow down during the test. Try taking a deep breath or counting to ten. As you read and consider the question, restrict yourself to the particular words used by the author. Avoid thought tangents about what the author *really* meant, or what he or she was *trying* to say. The only things that matter on a multiple-choice test are the words that are actually in the question. You must avoid reading too much into a multiple-choice question, or supposing that the writer meant something other than what he or she wrote.

5. No Need for Panic

It is wise to learn as many strategies as possible before taking a multiple-choice test, but it is likely that you will come across a few questions for which you simply don't know the answer. In this situation, avoid panicking. Because most multiple-choice tests include dozens of questions, the relative value of a single wrong answer is small. As much as possible, you should compartmentalize each question on a multiple-choice test. In other words, you should not allow your feelings about one question to affect your success on the others. When you find a question that you either don't understand or don't know how to answer, just take a deep breath and do your best. Read the entire question slowly and carefully. Try rephrasing the question a couple of different ways. Then, read all of the answer choices carefully. After eliminating obviously wrong answers, make a selection and move on to the next question.

6. Confusing Answer Choices

When working on a difficult multiple-choice question, there may be a tendency to focus on the answer choices that are the easiest to understand. Many people, whether consciously or not, gravitate to the answer choices that require the least concentration, knowledge, and memory. This is a mistake. When you come across an answer choice that is confusing, you should give it extra attention. A question might be confusing because you do not know the subject matter to which it refers. If this is the case, don't eliminate the answer before you have affirmatively settled on another. When you come across an answer choice of this type, set it aside as you look at the remaining choices. If you can confidently assert that one of the other choices is correct, you can leave the confusing answer aside. Otherwise, you will need to take a moment to try to better understand the confusing answer choice. Rephrasing is one way to tease out the sense of a confusing answer choice.

7. Your First Instinct

Many people struggle with multiple-choice tests because they overthink the questions. If you have studied sufficiently for the test, you should be prepared to trust your first instinct once you have carefully and completely read the question and all of the answer choices. There is a great deal of research suggesting that the mind can come to the correct conclusion very quickly once it has obtained all of the relevant information. At times, it may seem to you as if your intuition is working faster even than your reasoning mind. This may in fact be true. The knowledge you obtain while studying may be retrieved from your subconscious before you have a chance to work out the associations that support it. Verify your instinct by working out the reasons that it should be trusted.

8. Key Words

Many test takers struggle with multiple-choice questions because they have poor reading comprehension skills. Quickly reading and understanding a multiple-choice question requires a mixture of skill and experience. To help with this, try jotting down a few key words and phrases on a piece of scrap paper. Doing this concentrates the process of reading and forces the mind to weigh the relative importance of the question's parts. In selecting words and phrases to write down, the test taker thinks about the question more deeply and carefully. This is especially true for multiple-choice questions that are preceded by a long prompt.

9. Subtle Negatives

One of the oldest tricks in the multiple-choice test writer's book is to subtly reverse the meaning of a question with a word like *not* or *except*. If you are not paying attention to each word in the question, you can easily be led astray by this trick. For instance, a common question format is, "Which of the following is…?" Obviously, if the question instead is, "Which of the following is not…?," then the answer will be quite different. Even worse, the test makers are aware of the potential for this mistake and will include one answer choice that would be correct if the question were not negated or reversed. A test taker who misses the reversal will find what he or she believes to be a correct answer and will be so confident that he or she will fail to reread the question and discover the original error. The only way to avoid this is to practice a wide variety of multiple-choice questions and to pay close attention to each and every word.

10. Reading Every Answer Choice

It may seem obvious, but you should always read every one of the answer choices! Too many test takers fall into the habit of scanning the question and assuming that they understand the question because they recognize a few key words. From there, they pick the first answer choice that answers the question they believe they have read. Test takers who read all of the answer choices might discover that one of the latter answer choices is actually *more* correct. Moreover, reading all of the answer choices can remind you of facts related to the question that can help you arrive at the correct answer. Sometimes, a misstatement or incorrect detail in one of the latter answer choices will trigger your memory of the subject and will enable you to find the right answer. Failing to read all of the answer choices is like not reading all of the items on a restaurant menu: you might miss out on the perfect choice.

11. Spot the Hedges

One of the keys to success on multiple-choice tests is paying close attention to every word. This is never truer than with words like almost, most, some, and sometimes. These words are called "hedges" because they indicate that a statement is not totally true or not true in every place and time. An absolute statement will contain no hedges, but in many subjects, the answers are not always straightforward or absolute. There are always exceptions to the rules in these subjects. For this reason, you should favor those multiple-choice questions that contain hedging language. The presence of qualifying words indicates that the author is taking special care with his or her words, which is certainly important when composing the right answer. After all, there are many ways to be wrong, but there is only one way to be right! For this reason, it is wise to avoid answers that are absolute when taking a multiple-choice test. An absolute answer is one that says things are either all one way or all another. They often include words like *every*, *always*, *best*, and *never*. If you are taking a multiple-choice test in a subject that doesn't lend itself to absolute answers, be on your guard if you see any of these words.

12. Long Answers

In many subject areas, the answers are not simple. As already mentioned, the right answer often requires hedges. Another common feature of the answers to a complex or subjective question are qualifying clauses, which are groups of words that subtly modify the meaning of the sentence. If the question or answer choice describes a rule to which there are exceptions or the subject matter is complicated, ambiguous, or confusing, the correct answer will require many words in order to be expressed clearly and accurately. In essence, you should not be deterred by answer choices that seem excessively long. Oftentimes, the author of the text will not be able to write the correct answer without offering some qualifications and modifications. Your job is to read the answer choices thoroughly and completely and to select the one that most accurately and precisely answers the question.

13. Restating to Understand

Sometimes, a question on a multiple-choice test is difficult not because of what it asks but because of how it is written. If this is the case, restate the question or answer choice in different words. This process serves a couple of important purposes. First, it forces you to concentrate on the core of the question. In order to rephrase the question accurately, you have to understand it well. Rephrasing the question will concentrate your mind on the key words and ideas. Second, it will present the information to your mind in a fresh way. This process may trigger your memory and render some useful scrap of information picked up while studying.

14. True Statements

Sometimes an answer choice will be true in itself, but it does not answer the question. This is one of the main reasons why it is essential to read the question carefully and completely before proceeding to the answer choices. Too often, test takers skip ahead to the answer choices and look for true statements. Having found one of these, they are content to select it without reference to the question above. Obviously, this provides an easy way for test makers to play tricks. The savvy test taker will always read the entire question before turning to the answer choices. Then, having settled on a correct answer choice, he or she will refer to the original question and ensure that the selected answer is relevant. The mistake of choosing a correct-but-irrelevant answer choice is especially common on questions related to specific pieces of objective knowledge. A prepared test taker will have a wealth of factual knowledge at his or her disposal, and should not be careless in its application.

15. No Patterns

One of the more dangerous ideas that circulates about multiple-choice tests is that the correct answers tend to fall into patterns. These erroneous ideas range from a belief that B and C are the most common right answers, to the idea that an unprepared test-taker should answer "A-B-A-C-A-D-A-B-A." It cannot be emphasized enough that pattern-seeking of this type is exactly the WRONG way to approach a multiple-choice test. To begin with, it is highly unlikely that the test maker will plot the correct answers according to some predetermined pattern. The questions are scrambled and delivered in a random order. Furthermore, even if the test maker was following a pattern in the assignation of correct answers, there is no reason why the test taker would know which pattern he or she was using. Any attempt to discern a pattern in the answer choices is a waste of time and a distraction from the real work of taking the test. A test taker would be much better served by extra preparation before the test than by reliance on a pattern in the answers.

FREE DVD OFFER

Don't forget that doing well on your exam includes both understanding the test content and understanding how to use what you know to do well on the test. We offer a completely FREE Test Taking Tips DVD that covers world class test taking tips that you can use to be even more successful when you are taking your test.

All that we ask is that you email us your feedback about your study guide. To get your **FREE Test Taking Tips DVD**, email freedvd@studyguideteam.com with "FREE DVD" in the subject line and the following information in the body of the email:

- The title of your study guide.
- Your product rating on a scale of 1-5, with 5 being the highest rating.
- Your feedback about the study guide. What did you think of it?
- Your full name and shipping address to send your free DVD.

Introduction to the ACCUPLACER Exam

Function of the Test

ACCUPLACER is an adaptive, computerized test offered by the College Board and used by some colleges and high schools to determine placement of students in programs appropriate to the students' skill level. The test is offered nation-wide, at any college or high school that chooses to use it. Test-takers are almost always students of schools that use the ACCUPLACER in their course selection and placement efforts. Schools can also use the ACCUPLACER to assess students' skill levels and identify specific areas in which the students need improvement. Scores are generally used only by the college or high school the student is already attending for placement and instruction at that school.

According to the College Board, more than 1,500 secondary and post-secondary institutions are currently using the ACCUPLACER. Over 7.5 million ACCUPLACER tests are administered in a typical year. The College Board recommends that ACCUPLACER scores be used in conjunction with other variables including high school GPA, the number of years a student has taken coursework in a particular subject area, other test scores such as the SAT or ACT, as well as non-cognitive information such as motivation, family support, and time management skills, in order to place students in courses of appropriate difficulty.

Test Administration

ACCUPLACER is offered by computer, usually by the school that wants to use its results, whenever a student makes an appointment with the school to take it. In cases where a student is not able to take the test at the student's school, arrangements can sometimes be made to take the test at a more convenient location on another school's campus.

Fees for taking the ACCUPLACER vary from school to school. Students sometimes do not pay a fee at all; rather, the school pays the College Board for the right to administer the test and then students take it for free. Students may retake the ACCUPLACER at the discretion of the school administering the test and using its results. Students with documented disabilities can make arrangements, through the test center offering the ACCUPLACER, to take the test with appropriate accommodations, including the potential availability of a written version of the test.

Test Format

The core of the ACCUPLACER is five multiple-choice subject area tests: Arithmetic, College-level Math, Elementary Algebra, Reading Comprehension, and Sentence Skills. A college may ask a student to test in any or all of the five subject areas, depending on the student's and the school's needs. There is also a sixth section, called the WritePlacer, in which students must write a brief essay. Finally, there are four multiple-choice ESL sections of the ACCUPLACER, which schools may ask students, for whom English is a second language, to take.

The multiple-choice sections of the ACCUPLACER are administered by computer. There is no time-limit, so test takers should feel free to work at their own pace. A typical test section might take around 30 minutes to complete. The test is adaptive, meaning it adjusts the difficulty of each question based on the student's success on the previous questions. The more questions a test-taker gets right, the harder succeeding questions will be and vice-versa. This allows the test to more readily determine test-takers' ability levels without wasting time on questions far above or far below what the test-takers can answer.

Section	Questions	Description
Arithmetic	17	Basic arithmetic and problem solving
College Level Math	20	Algebra, geometry, trigonometry
Elementary Algebra	12	Basic algebra
Reading Comprehension	20	Understanding reading; making inferences
Sentence Skills	20	Sentence structure; relationships between sentences
WritePlacer	1 essay	Effective written communication
ESL- Language Use	20	English grammar
ESL- Listening	20	Understanding spoken English communication
ESL- Reading Skills	20	Comprehension of short written English passages
ESL- Sentence Meaning	20	Understanding the meaning of English sentences

Scoring

The ACCUPLACER subject area tests are scored on a scale from 20 to 120. Schools are free to use the scores for placement as they see fit, given that the difficulty of coursework varies from school to school. A typical community college might separate scores into tiered groups from 50 to 75, from 75 to 99, and from 100 to 120. Scores are typically generated instantly by the computer, but may not be available from the school administering the test until the school has had a chance to review the scores and use them for placement purposes.

Recent/Future Developments

Starting in September 2016, the College Board will be making "next-generation" ACCUPLACER tests available to schools. Schools will have the option of administering the next-generation tests or the older tests, but not both. The new next-generation tests will include redesigned reading, writing, and math content, intended to more effectively help schools place students in classes that match their skill level.

Reading Comprehension

Central Ideas and Themes

Topic, Main Idea, Supporting Details, and Themes

The **topic** of a text is the overall subject, and the **main idea** more specifically builds on that subject. Consider a paragraph that begins with the following: "The United States government is made of up three branches: executive, judicial, and legislative." If this sentence is divided into its essential components, there is the topic (United States Government) and the main idea (the three branches of government).

A main idea must be supported with details, which usually appear in the form of quotations, paraphrasing, or analysis. Authors should connect details and analysis to the main point. Readers should always be cautious when accepting the validity of an argument and look for logical fallacies, such as slippery slope, straw man, and begging the question. While arguments may seem sound, further analysis often reveals they are flawed. It's okay for a reader to disagree with an author.

It is important to remember that when most authors write, they want to make a point or send a message. This point or the message of a text is known as the **theme**. Authors may state themes explicitly, like in *Aesop's Fables*. More often, especially in modern literature, readers must infer the theme based on textual details. Usually after carefully reading and analyzing an entire text, the theme emerges. Typically, the longer the piece, the more numerous its themes, though often one theme dominates the rest, as evidenced by the author's purposeful revisiting of it throughout the passage.

Cultural Differences in Themes

Regardless of culture, place, or time, certain themes are universal to the human condition. Because all humans experience certain feelings and engage in similar experiences—birth, death, marriage, friendship, finding meaning, etc.—certain themes span cultures. However, different cultures have different norms and general beliefs concerning these themes. For example, the theme of maturing and crossing from childhood to adulthood is a global theme; however, the literature from one culture might imply that this happens in someone's twenties, while another culture's literature might imply that it happens in the early teenage years.

It's important for the reader to be aware of these differences. Readers must avoid being **ethnocentric**, which means believing the aspects of one's own culture to be superior to those of other cultures.

Summarizing Information Accurately

Analyzing Topics and Summary Sentences

Good writers get to the point quickly. This is accomplished by developing a strong and effective topic sentence that details the author's purpose and answers questions such as: *What does the author intend to explain or impress?* or *What does the author want the reader to believe?* The **topic sentence** is normally found at the beginning of a supporting paragraph and usually gives purpose to a single paragraph. When reading, critical readers should find the topic sentence in each paragraph. If all information points back to one sentence, it's the topic sentence.

Summary sentences offer a recap of previously discussed information before transitioning to the next point or proceeding to the closing thoughts. Summary sentences can be found at the end of supporting paragraphs and in the conclusion of a text.

Drawing Logical Inferences and Conclusions

Identifying Logical Conclusions

Determining conclusions requires being an active reader, as a reader must make a prediction and analyze facts to identify a conclusion. A reader should identify key words in a passage to determine the logical conclusion from the information presented. Consider the passage below:

> Lindsay, covered in flour, moved around the kitchen frantically. Her mom yelled from another room, "Lindsay, we're going to be late!

Readers can conclude that Lindsay's next steps are to finish baking, clean herself up, and head off somewhere with her baked goods. It's important to note that the conclusion cannot be verified factually. Many conclusions are not spelled out specifically in the text; thus, they have to be inferred and deduced by the reader.

Evaluating a Passage

Readers draw **conclusions** about what an author has presented. This helps them better understand what the writer has intended to communicate and whether or not they agree with what the author has offered. There are a few ways to determine a logical conclusion, but careful reading is the most important. It's helpful to read a passage a few times, noting details that seem important to the piece. Sometimes, readers arrive at a conclusion that is different than what the writer intended or they may come up with more than one conclusion.

Textual evidence within the details helps readers draw a conclusion about a passage. **Textual evidence** refers to information—facts and examples—that support the main point. Textual evidence will likely come from outside sources and can be in the form of quoted or paraphrased material. In order to draw a conclusion from evidence, it's important to examine the credibility and validity of that evidence as well as how (and if) it relates to the main idea.

If an author presents a differing opinion or a **counterargument**, in order to refute it, the reader should consider how and why this information is being presented. It is meant to strengthen the original argument and shouldn't be confused with the author's intended conclusion, but it should also be considered in the reader's final evaluation.

Sometimes, authors explicitly state the conclusion that they want readers to understand. Alternatively, a conclusion may not be directly stated. In that case, readers must rely on the implications to form a logical conclusion:

> On the way to the bus stop, Michael realized his homework wasn't in his backpack. He ran back to the house to get it and made it back to the bus just in time.

In this example, although it's never explicitly stated, it can be inferred that Michael is a student on his way to school in the morning. When forming a conclusion from implied information, it's important to read the text carefully to find several pieces of evidence in the text to support the conclusion.

Summarizing is an effective way to draw a conclusion from a passage. A **summary** is a shortened version of the original text, written by the reader in his or her own words. Focusing on the main points of the original text and including only the relevant details can help readers reach a conclusion. It's important to retain the original meaning of the passage.

Like summarizing, **paraphrasing** can also help a reader fully understand different parts of a text. Paraphrasing calls for the reader to take a small part of the passage and list or describe its main points. However, paraphrasing is more than rewording the original passage; it should be written in the reader's own words, while still retaining the meaning of the original source. This will indicate an understanding of the original source, yet still help the reader expand on his or her interpretation.

Word and Phrase Meanings

Most experts agree that learning new words is worth the time it takes. It helps readers understand what they are reading, and it expands their vocabularies. An extensive vocabulary improves one's ability to think. When words are added to someone's vocabulary, he or she is better able to make sense of the world.

One of the fastest ways to decode a word is through context. **Context**, or surrounding words, gives clues as to what unknown words mean. Take the following example: *When the students in the classroom teased Johnny, he was so discombobulated that he couldn't finish a simple math problem.* Even though a reader might be unfamiliar with the word *discombobulated*, he or she can use context clues in the sentence to make sense of the word. In this case, it can be deduced that *discombobulated* means confused or distracted.

Although context clues provide a rudimentary understanding of a word, using a dictionary can provide the reader with a more comprehensive meaning of the word. Printed dictionaries list words in alphabetical order, and all versions—including those online—include a word's multiple meanings. Typically, the first definition is the most widely used or known. The second, third, and subsequent entries move toward the more unusual or archaic. Dictionaries also indicate the part(s) of speech of each word, such as noun, verb, adjective, etc.

Dictionaries are not fixed in time. The English language today looks nothing like it did in Shakespeare's time, and Shakespeare's English is vastly different from Chaucer's. The English language is constantly evolving, as evidenced by the deletion of old words and the addition of new ones. *Ginormous* and *bling-bling*, for example, can both be found in *Merriam-Webster's* latest edition, yet they were not found in prior editions.

Determining the Denotative Meaning of Words

Connotation refers to the implied meaning of a word or phrase. Connotations are the ideas or feelings that words or phrase invoke other than their literal meaning. An example of the use of connotation is in people's use of the word *cheap*. While the literal meaning is something of low cost, people use the word to suggest something is poor in value or to negatively describe a person as reluctant to spend money. When something or someone is described this way, the reader is more inclined to have a particular image or feeling about it or him/her. Thus, connotation can be a very effective language tool in creating emotion and swaying opinion. However, connotations are sometimes hard to pin down because varying emotions can be associated with a word. Generally, though, connotative meanings tend to be fairly consistent within a specific cultural group.

Denotation is the literal definition of a word or phrase. The denotative meaning of a word is the one you would find in a dictionary. To present hard facts or vocabulary terms, it is helpful for a writer to use words which are mainly known for their denotative meanings rather than their connotative ones. In those instances, the words *inexpensive* and *frugal* are better because they do not carry the negative connotations that cheap does. *Inexpensive* refers to the cost of something, not its value, and *frugal* indicates that a person is conscientiously watching his or her spending. These terms do not elicit the same emotions that *cheap* does.

Authors sometimes choose to use both, but what they choose and when they use it is what critical readers need to differentiate. One method isn't inherently better than the other; however, one may create a better effect, depending upon an author's intent. If, for example, an author's purpose is to inform, to instruct, and to familiarize readers with a difficult subject, his or her use of connotation may be helpful. However, it may also undermine credibility and confuse readers. An author who wants to create a credible, scholarly effect in his or her text would most likely use denotation, which emphasizes literal, factual meaning and examples.

Use a dictionary to find the denotative meaning of words. Though context clues provide a rudimentary understanding of a word, using a dictionary can provide the reader with a more comprehensive meaning of the word. Printed dictionaries list words in alphabetical order, and all versions, including those online, include a word's multiples meanings. Typically, the first definition is the most widely used or known. The second, third, and subsequent entries move toward the more unusual or archaic. Dictionaries also indicate the part of speech of each word, such as noun, verb, adjective, etc.

Keep in mind that dictionaries are not fixed in time. The English language today looks nothing like it did in Shakespeare's time, and Shakespeare's English is vastly different from Chaucer's. The English language is constantly evolving, as evidenced by the deletion of old words and the addition of new. *Ginormous* and *bling-bling*, for example, can both be found in *Merriam-Webster's* latest edition.

Analyzing an Author's Rhetorical Choices

Authors utilize a wide range of techniques to tell a story or communicate information. Readers should be familiar with the most common of these techniques. Techniques of writing are also known as **rhetorical devices**.

In nonfiction writing, authors employ argumentative techniques to present their opinions to readers in the most convincing way. First of all, persuasive writing usually includes at least one type of **appeal**: an appeal to logic (**logos**), emotion (**pathos**), or credibility and trustworthiness (**ethos**). When writers appeal to logic, they are asking readers to agree with them based on research, evidence, and an established line of reasoning. An author's argument might also appeal to readers' emotions, perhaps by including personal stories and **anecdotes** (a short narrative of a specific event). A final type of appeal—appeal to authority—asks the reader to agree with the author's argument on the basis of their expertise or credentials. Three different approaches to arguing the same opinion are exemplified below:

<u>Logic (Logos)</u>

> Our school should abolish its current ban on cell phone use on campus. This rule was adopted last year as an attempt to reduce class disruptions and help students focus more on their lessons. However, since the rule was enacted, there has been no change in the number of disciplinary problems in class. Therefore, the rule is ineffective and should be done away with.

The above is an example of an appeal to logic. The author uses evidence to disprove the logic of the school's rule (the rule was supposed to reduce discipline problems; the number of problems has not been reduced; therefore, the rule is not working) and to call for its repeal.

Emotion (Pathos)

An author's argument might also appeal to readers' emotions, perhaps by including personal stories and anecdotes.

The next example presents an appeal to emotion. By sharing the personal anecdote of one student and speaking about emotional topics like family relationships, the author invokes the reader's empathy in asking them to reconsider the school rule.

> Our school should abolish its current ban on cell phone use on campus. If they aren't able to use their phones during the school day, many students feel isolated from their loved ones. For example, last semester, one student's grandmother had a heart attack in the morning. However, because he couldn't use his cell phone, the student didn't know about his grandmother's accident until the end of the day—when she had already passed away and it was too late to say goodbye. By preventing students from contacting their friends and family, our school is placing undue stress and anxiety on students.

Credibility (Ethos)

Finally, an appeal to authority includes a statement from a relevant expert. In this case, the author uses a doctor in the field of education to support the argument. All three examples begin from the same opinion—the school's phone ban needs to change—but rely on different argumentative styles to persuade the reader.

> Our school should abolish its current ban on cell phone use on campus. According to Dr. Bartholomew Everett, a leading educational expert, "Research studies show that cell phone usage has no real impact on student attentiveness. Rather, phones provide a valuable technological resource for learning. Schools need to learn how to integrate this new technology into their curriculum." Rather than banning phones altogether, our school should follow the advice of experts and allow students to use phones as part of their learning.

Rhetorical Questions

Another commonly used argumentative technique is asking **rhetorical questions**, which are questions that do not actually require an answer but that push the reader to consider the topic further.

> I wholly disagree with the proposal to ban restaurants from serving foods with high sugar and sodium contents. Do we really want to live in a world where the government can control what we eat? I prefer to make my own food choices.

Here, the author's rhetorical question prompts readers to put themselves in a hypothetical situation and imagine how they would feel about it.

Figurative Language

Similes and **metaphors** are part of figurative language that are used as rhetorical devices. Both are comparisons between two things, but their formats differ slightly. A simile says that two things are similar and makes a comparison using "like" or "as"—*A* is like *B,* or *A* is as [some characteristic] as *B*—whereas a metaphor states that two things are exactly the same—*A* is *B*. In both cases, similes and metaphors invite the reader to think more deeply about the characteristics of the two subjects and consider where they overlap. Sometimes the poet develops a complex metaphor throughout the entire poem; this is known as an extended metaphor. An example of metaphor can be found in the sentence:

"His pillow was a fluffy cloud". An example of simile can be found in the first line of Robert Burns' famous poem:

My love is like a red, red rose

This is comparison using "like," and the two things being compared are love and a rose. Some characteristics of a rose are that it is fragrant, beautiful, blossoming, colorful, vibrant—by comparing his love to a red, red rose, Burns asks the reader to apply these qualities of a rose to his love. In this way, he implies that his love is also fresh, blossoming, and brilliant.

In addition to rhetorical devices that play on the *meanings* of words, there are also rhetorical devices that use the sounds of words. These devices are most often found in poetry, but may also be found in other types of literature and in nonfiction writing like texts for speeches.

Alliteration and **assonance** are both varieties of sound repetition. Other types of sound repetition include: **anaphora**—repetition that occurs at the beginning of the sentences; **epiphora**—repetition occurring at the end of phrases; antimetabole—repetition of words in a succession; and antiphrasis—a form of denial of an assertion in a text.

Alliteration refers to the repetition of the first sound of each word. Recall Robert Burns' opening line:

My love is like a red, red rose

This line includes two instances of alliteration: "love" and "like" (repeated *L* sound), as well as "red" and "rose" (repeated *R* sound). Next, assonance refers to the repetition of vowel sounds, and can occur anywhere within a word (not just the opening sound). Here is the opening of a poem by John Keats:

When I have fears that I may cease to be

Before my pen has glean'd my teeming brain

Assonance can be found in the words "fears," "cease," "be," "glean'd," and "teeming," all of which stress the long *E* sound. Both alliteration and assonance create a harmony that unifies the writer's language.

Another sound device is **onomatopoeia**—words whose spelling mimics the sound they describe. Words like "crash," "bang," and "sizzle" are all examples of onomatopoeia. Use of onomatopoetic language adds auditory imagery to the text.

Readers are probably most familiar with the technique of using a **pun**. A pun is a play on words, taking advantage of two words that have the same or similar pronunciation. Puns can be found throughout Shakespeare's plays, for instance:

Now is the winter of our discontent

Made glorious summer by this son of York

These lines from *Richard III* contain a play on words. Richard III refers to his brother—the newly crowned King Edward IV—as the "son of York," referencing their family heritage from the house of York. However, while drawing a comparison between the political climate and the weather (times of political trouble were the "winter," but now the new king brings "glorious summer"), Richard's use of the word "son" also implies another word with the same pronunciation, "sun"—so Edward IV is also like the sun, bringing light, warmth, and hope to England. Puns are a clever way for writers to suggest two meanings at once.

Analyzing Text Structure

Analyzing and Evaluating Text Structure

Depending on what the author is attempting to accomplish, certain formats or text structures work better than others. For example, a sequence structure might work for narration but not when identifying similarities and differences between dissimilar concepts. Similarly, a comparison-contrast structure is not useful for narration. It's the author's job to put the right information in the correct format.

Readers should be familiar with the five main literary structures:

1. **Sequence** structure (sometimes referred to as the order structure) is when the order of events proceeds in a predictable manner. In many cases, this means the text goes through the plot elements: exposition, rising action, climax, falling action, and resolution. Readers are introduced to characters, setting, and conflict in the exposition. In the rising action, there's an increase in tension and suspense. The climax is the height of tension and the point of no return. Tension decreases during the falling action. In the resolution, any conflicts presented in the exposition are solved, and the story concludes. An informative text that is structured sequentially will often go in order from one step to the next.

2. In the **problem-solution** structure, authors identify a potential problem and suggest a solution. This form of writing is usually divided into two paragraphs and can be found in informational texts. For example, cell phone, cable and satellite providers use this structure in manuals to help customers troubleshoot or identify problems with services or products.

3. When authors want to discuss similarities and differences between separate concepts, they arrange thoughts in a **comparison-contrast** paragraph structure. **Venn diagrams** are an effective graphic organizer for comparison-contrast structures, because they feature two overlapping circles that can be used to organize and group similarities and differences. A comparison-contrast essay organizes one paragraph based on similarities and another based on differences. A comparison-contrast essay can also be arranged with the similarities and differences of individual traits addressed within individual paragraphs. Words such as *however*, *but*, and *nevertheless* help signal a contrast in ideas.

4. The **descriptive** writing structure is designed to appeal to one's senses. Much like an artist who constructs a painting, good descriptive writing builds an image in the reader's mind by appealing to the five senses: sight, hearing, taste, touch, and smell. However, overly descriptive writing can become tedious; sparse descriptions can make settings and characters seem flat. Good authors strike a balance by applying descriptions only to passages, characters, and settings that are integral to the plot.

5. Passages that use the **cause and effect** structure are simply asking *why* by demonstrating some type of connection between ideas. Words such as *if*, *since*, *because*, *then*, or *consequently* indicate relationship. By switching the order of a complex sentence, the writer can rearrange the emphasis on different clauses. Saying *If Sheryl is late, we'll miss the dance* is different from saying, *We'll miss the dance if Sheryl is late*. One emphasizes Sheryl's tardiness while the other emphasizes missing the dance. Paragraphs can also be arranged in a cause and effect format. Since the format—before and after—is

sequential, it is useful when authors wish to discuss the impact of choices. Researchers often apply this paragraph structure to the scientific method.

Authorial Purpose and Perspective

No matter the genre or format, all authors are writing to persuade, inform, entertain, or express feelings. Often, these purposes are blended, with one dominating the rest. It's useful to learn to recognize the author's intent.

Persuasive writing is used to persuade or convince readers of something. It often contains two elements: the argument and the counterargument. The **argument** takes a stance on an issue, while the **counterargument** pokes holes in the opposition's stance. Authors rely on logic, emotion, and writer credibility to persuade readers to agree with them. If readers are opposed to the stance before reading, they are unlikely to adopt that stance. However, those who are undecided or committed to the same stance are more likely to agree with the author.

Informative writing tries to teach or inform. Workplace manuals, instructor lessons, statistical reports and cookbooks are examples of informative texts. Informative writing is usually based on facts and is often without emotion and persuasion. Informative texts generally contain statistics, charts, and graphs. Although most informative texts lack a persuasive agenda, readers must examine the text carefully to determine whether one exists within a given passage.

Stories or **narratives** are designed to entertain. When people go to the movies, they often want to escape for a few hours, not necessarily to think critically. **Entertaining** writing is designed to delight and engage the reader. However, sometimes this type of writing can be woven into more serious materials, such as persuasive or informative writing, to hook the reader before transitioning into a more scholarly discussion.

Emotional writing works to evoke the reader's feelings, such as anger, euphoria, or sadness. The connection between reader and author is an attempt to cause the reader to share the author's intended emotion or tone. Sometimes, in order to make a text more poignant, the author simply wants readers to feel the emotions that the author has felt. Other times, the author attempts to persuade or manipulate the reader into adopting their stance. While it's okay to sympathize with the author, readers should be aware of the individual's underlying intent.

Evaluating the Author's Point of View in a Given Text

When it comes to authors' writings, readers should always identify a position or stance. No matter how objective a piece may seem, assume the author has preconceived beliefs. Reduce the likelihood of accepting an invalid argument by looking for multiple articles on the topic, including those with varying opinions. If several opinions point in the same direction, and are backed by reputable peer-reviewed sources, it's more likely the author has a valid argument. Positions that run contrary to widely held beliefs and existing data should invite scrutiny. There are exceptions to the rule, so be a careful consumer of information.

Though themes, symbols, and motifs are buried deep within the text and can sometimes be difficult to infer, an author's purpose is usually obvious from the beginning. There are four purposes of writing: to inform, to persuade, to describe, and to entertain. Informative writings present facts in an accessible way. Persuasive writing is appeals to emotions and logic to inspire the reader to adopt a specific stance. Be wary of this type of writing, as it often lacks objectivity. Descriptive writing is designed to paint a picture in the reader's mind, while writings that entertain are often narratives designed to engage and delight the reader.

The various writing styles are usually blended, with one purpose dominating the rest. For example, a persuasive piece might begin with a humorous tale to make readers more receptive to the persuasive message, or a recipe in a cookbook designed to inform might be preceded by an entertaining anecdote that makes the recipe more appealing.

Analyzing Characters' Points of View

<u>Point of View</u>
Point of view is another important writing device to consider. In fiction writing, **point of view** refers to who tells the story or from whose perspective readers are observing as they read. In nonfiction writing, the **point of view** refers to whether the author refers to himself or herself, his or her readers, or chooses not to refer to either. Whether fiction or nonfiction, the author carefully considers the impact the perspective will have on the purpose and main point of the writing.

- **First-person** point of view: The story is told from the writer's perspective. In fiction, this would mean that the main character is also the narrator. First-person point of view is easily recognized by the use of personal pronouns such as *I, me, we, us, our, my*, and *myself*.
- **Third-person** point of view: In a more formal essay, this would be an appropriate perspective because the focus should be on the subject matter, not the writer or the reader. Third-person point of view is recognized by the use of the pronouns *he, she, they*, and *it*. In fiction writing, third person point of view has a few variations.
    - ***Third-person limited*** point of view refers to a story told by a narrator who has access to the thoughts and feelings of just one character.
    - In **third-person omniscient** point of view, the narrator has access to the thoughts and feelings of all the characters.
    - In **third-person objective** point of view, the narrator is like a fly on the wall and can see and hear what the characters do and say but does not have access to their thoughts and feelings.
- **Second-person** point of view: This point of view isn't commonly used in fiction or nonfiction writing because it directly addresses the reader using the pronouns *you, your*, and *yourself*. Second-person perspective is more appropriate in direct communication, such as business letters or emails.

Point of View	Pronouns used
First person	I, me, we, us, our, my, myself
Second person	You, your, yourself
Third person	He, she, it, they

Interpreting Authorial Decisions Rhetorically

There are a few ways for readers to engage actively with the text, such as making inferences and predictions. An **inference** refers to a point that is implied (as opposed to directly-stated) by the evidence presented:

> Bradley packed up all of the items from his desk in a box and said goodbye to his coworkers for the last time.

From this sentence, although it is not directly stated, readers can infer that Bradley is leaving his job. It's necessary to use inference in order to draw conclusions about the meaning of a passage. When making an inference about a passage, it's important to rely only on the information that is provided in the text itself. This helps readers ensure that their conclusions are valid.

Readers will also find themselves making predictions when reading a passage or paragraph. **Predictions** are guesses about what's going to happen next. This is a natural tendency, especially when reading a good story or watching a suspenseful movie. It's fun to try to figure out how it will end. Authors intentionally use suspenseful language and situations to keep readers interested:

> A cat darted across the street just as the car came careening around the curve.

One unfortunate prediction might be that the car will hit the cat. Of course, predictions aren't always accurate, so it's important to read carefully to the end of the text to determine the accuracy of one's predictions.

Readers should pay attention to the **sequence**, or the order in which details are laid out in the text, as this can be important to understanding its meaning as a whole. Writers will often use transitional words to help the reader understand the order of events and to stay on track. Words like *next, then, after,* and *finally* show that the order of events is important to the author. In some cases, the author omits these transitional words, and the sequence is implied. Authors may even purposely present the information out of order to make an impact or have an effect on the reader. An example might be when a narrative writer uses **flashback** to reveal information.

Drawing conclusions is also important when actively reading a passage. **Hedge phrases** such as *will, might, probably,* and *appear to be* are used by writers who want to cover their bases and make sure to show there are exceptions to their statements. **Absolute phrasing**, such as *always* and *never*, should be carefully considered, as the use of these words and their intended meanings are often incorrect.

Differentiating Between Various Perspectives and Sources of Information

Identifying the Appropriate Source for Locating Information

With a wealth of information at people's fingertips in this digital age, it's important to know not only the type of information one is looking for, but also in what medium he or she is most likely to find it. Information needs to be specific and reliable. For example, if someone is repairing a car, an encyclopedia would be mostly useless. While an encyclopedia might include information about cars, an owner's manual will contain the specific information needed for repairs. Information must also be reliable or credible so that it can be trusted. A well-known newspaper may have reliable information, but a peer-reviewed journal article will have likely gone through a more rigorous check for validity. Determining **bias** can be helpful in determining credibility. If the information source (person, organization, or company) has something to gain from the reader forming a certain view on a topic, it's likely the information is skewed. For example, if trying to find the unemployment rate, the Bureau of Labor Statistics is a more credible source than a politician's speech.

Primary sources are best defined as records or items that serve as evidence of periods of history. To be considered primary, the source documents or objects must have been created during the time period in which they reference. Examples include diaries, newspaper articles, speeches, government documents, photographs, and historical artifacts. In today's digital age, primary sources, which were once in print, are often embedded in secondary sources. **Secondary sources**—such as websites, history books, databases, or reviews—contain analysis or commentary on primary sources. Secondary sources borrow information from primary sources through the process of quoting, summarizing, or paraphrasing.

Today's students often complete research online through **electronic sources**. Electronic sources offer advantages over print, and can be accessed on virtually any computer, where libraries or other research centers are limited to fixed locations and specific catalogs. Electronic sources are also efficient and yield massive amounts of data in seconds. The user can tailor a search based on key words, publication years, and article length. Lastly, many **databases** provide the user with instant citations, saving the user the trouble of manually assembling sources for a bibliography.

Although electronic sources yield powerful results, researchers must use caution. While there are many reputable and reliable sources on the internet, just as many are unreliable or biased sources. It's up to the researcher to examine and verify the reliability of sources. *Wikipedia*, for example, may or may not be accurate, depending on the contributor. Many databases, such as *EBSCO* or *SIRS*, offer peer-reviewed articles, meaning the publications have been reviewed for the quality and accuracy of their content.

Understanding Authors' Claims

The goal of most persuasive and informative texts is to make a claim and support it with evidence. A **claim** is a statement made as though it is fact. Many claims are opinions; for example, "stealing is wrong." While this is generally true, it is arguable, meaning it is capable of being challenged. An initial reaction to "stealing is wrong" might be to agree; however, there may be circumstances in which it is warranted. If it is necessary for the survival of an individual or their loved ones (i.e., if they are starving and cannot afford to eat), then this assertion becomes morally ambiguous. While it may still be illegal, whether it is "wrong" is unclear.

When an assertion is made within a text, it is typically reinforced with supporting details as is exemplified in the following passage:

> The extinction of the dinosaurs has been a hot debate amongst scientists since the discovery of fossils in the eighteenth century. Numerous theories were developed in explanation, including extreme climate change, an epidemic of disease, or changes in the atmosphere. It wasn't until the late 1970s that a young geochemist, named Walter Alvarez, noticed significant changes in the soil layers of limestone he was studying in Italy. The layers contained fossilized remains of millions of small organisms within the layer that corresponded with the same period in which the dinosaurs lived. He noticed that the soil layer directly above this layer was suddenly devoid of any trace of these organisms. The soil layer directly above *this* layer was filled with an entirely new species of organisms. It seemed the first species had disappeared at the exact same time as the dinosaurs!

> With the help of his father, Walter Alvarez analyzed the soil layer between the extinct species and the new species and realized this layer was filled with an abnormal amount of *iridium* – a substance that is abundant in meteorites but almost never found on Earth. Unlike other elements in the fossil record, which take a long time to deposit, the iridium had been laid down very abruptly. The layer also contained high levels of soot, enough to account for all of the earth's forests burning to the ground at the same time. This lead scientists to create the best-supported theory that the tiny organisms, as well as the dinosaurs and countless other species, had been destroyed by a giant asteroid that had slammed into Earth, raining tons of iridium down on the planet from a giant cosmic cloud.

Supporting Claims

Before embarking on answering these questions, readers should summarize each. This will help in locating the supporting evidence. These summaries can be written down or completed mentally; full sentences are not necessary.

Paragraph 1: Layer of limestone shows that a species of organisms disappeared at same time as the dinosaurs

Paragraph 2: Layer had high amounts of iridium and soot – scientists believe dinosaurs destroyed by asteroid.

Simply by summarizing the text, it has been plainly outlined where there will be answers to relevant questions. Although there are often claims already embedded within an educational text, a claim will most likely be given, but the evidence to support it will need to be located. Take this example question:

> Q: What evidence within the text best supports the theory that the dinosaurs became extinct because of an asteroid?

The claim here is that the dinosaurs went extinct because of an asteroid. Because the text is already outlined in the summaries, it is easy to see that the evidence supporting this theory is in the second paragraph:

> With the help of his father, they analyzed the soil layer between the extinct species and the new species and realized this layer was filled with an abnormal amount of *iridium* – a substance that is abundant is meteorites but almost never found on Earth. Unlike other elements in the fossil record, which takes a long time to deposit, the iridium had been laid down very abruptly. The layer also contained high levels of soot, enough to account for all of the earth's forests burning to the ground at the same time. This lead scientists to create the best-supported theory that the tiny organisms, as well as the dinosaurs and countless other species, had been destroyed by a giant asteroid that had slammed into Earth, raining tons of iridium down on the planet from a giant cosmic cloud.

Now that the evidence within the text that best supports the theory has been located, the answer choices can be evaluated:

a. Changes in climate and atmosphere caused an asteroid to crash into Earth
b. Walter and Luis Alvarez studied limestone with fossilized organisms
c. A soil layer lacking organisms that existed at the same time as the dinosaurs showed low levels of iridium
d. A soil layer lacking organisms that existed at the same time as the dinosaurs showed high levels of iridium

Answer choice (a) is clearly false as there is nothing within the text that claims that climate changes caused an asteroid to crash into Earth. This kind of answer choice displays an incorrect use of detail. Although the passage may have contained the words "change," "climate," and "atmosphere," these terms were manipulated to form an erroneous answer.

Answer choice (b) is incorrect because while the scientists did study limestone with fossilized organisms, and in doing so they discovered evidence that led to the formation of the theory, this is not the actual evidence itself. This is an example of an out-of-scope answer choice: a true statement that may or may not have been in the passage, but that isn't the whole answer or isn't the point.

Answer choice (c) is incorrect because it is the opposite of the correct answer. Assuming the second paragraph was summarized correctly, it is already known that the soil layer contained *high* levels of iridium, not low levels. Even if the paragraph was not summarized that way, the final sentence states that "tons of iridium rained down on the planet." So, answer choice (c) is false.

Answer choice (d) is correct because it matches the evidence found in the second paragraph.

Differentiating Between Facts and Opinions

Fact and Opinion, Biases, and Stereotypes

It is important to distinguish between facts and opinions when reading a piece of writing. When an author presents **facts**, such as statistics or data, readers should be able to check those facts to verify that they are accurate. When authors share their own thoughts and feelings about a subject, they are expressing their **opinions**.

Authors often use words like *think, feel, believe,* or *in my opinion* when expressing an opinion, but these words won't always appear in an opinion piece, especially if it is formally written. An author's opinion may be backed up by facts, which gives it more credibility, but that opinion should not be taken as fact. A critical reader should be suspect of an author's opinion, especially if it is only supported by other opinions.

Fact	Opinion
There are nine innings in a game of baseball.	Baseball games run too long.
James Garfield was assassinated on July 2, 1881.	James Garfield was a good president.
McDonald's® has stores in 118 countries.	McDonald's® has the best hamburgers.

Critical readers examine the facts used to support an author's argument. They check the facts against other sources to be sure those facts are correct. They also check the validity of the sources used to be sure those sources are credible, academic, and/or peer-reviewed. When an author uses another person's opinion to support his or her argument, even if it is an expert's opinion, it is still only an opinion and should not be taken as fact. A strong argument uses valid, measurable facts to support ideas. Even then, the reader may disagree with the argument.

An authoritative argument may use the facts to sway the reader. In the example of global warming, many experts differ in their opinions of which alternative fuels can be used to aid in offsetting it. Because of this, a writer may choose to only use the information and experts' opinions that supports his or her viewpoint. For example, if the argument is that wind energy is the best solution, the author will use facts that support this idea. That same author may leave out relevant facts on solar energy. The way the author uses facts can influence the reader, so it's important to consider the facts being used, how those facts are being presented, and what information might be left out.

Authors can also demonstrate **bias** if they ignore an opposing viewpoint or present their side in an unbalanced way. A strong argument considers the opposition and finds a way to refute it. Critical readers should look for an unfair or one-sided presentation of the argument and be skeptical, as a bias may be present. Even if this bias is unintentional, if it exists in the writing, the reader should be wary of the validity of the argument.

Readers should also look for the use of stereotypes that refer to specific groups. **Stereotypes** are often negative connotations about a person or place and should always be avoided. When a critical reader finds stereotypes in a piece of writing, he or she should immediately be critical of the argument and consider the validity of anything the author presents. Stereotypes reveal a flaw in the writer's thinking and may suggest a lack of knowledge or understanding about the subject.

Using Evidence to Make Connections Between Different Texts

When analyzing two or more texts, there are several different aspects that need to be considered, particularly the styles (or the artful way in which the authors use diction to deliver a theme), points of view, and types of argument. In order to do so, one should compare and contrast the following elements between the texts:

- Style: narrative, persuasive, descriptive, informative, etc.
- Tone: sarcastic, angry, somber, humorous, etc.
- Sentence structure: simple (1 clause) compound (2 clauses), complex-compound (3 clauses)
- Punctuation choice: question marks, exclamation points, periods, dashes, etc.
- Point of view: first person, second person, third person
- Paragraph structure: long, short, both, differences between the two
- Organizational structure: compare/contrast, problem/solution, chronological, etc.

The following two passages concern the theme of death and are presented to demonstrate how to evaluate the above elements:

Passage I

Death occurs in several stages. The first stage is the pre-active stage, which occurs a few days to weeks before death, in which the desire to eat and drink decreases, and the person may feel restless, irritable, and anxious. The second stage is the active stage, where the skin begins to cool, breathing becomes difficult as the lungs become congested (known as the "death rattle"), and the person loses control of their bodily fluids.

Once death occurs, there are also two stages. The first is clinical death, when the heart stops pumping blood and breathing ceases. This stage lasts approximately 4-6 minutes, and during this time, it is possible for a victim to be resuscitated via CPR or a defibrillator. After 6 minutes however, the oxygen stores within the brain begin to deplete, and the victim enters biological death. This is the point of no return, as the cells of the brain and vital organs begin to die, a process that is irreversible.

Passage II

It was her sister Josephine who told her, in broken sentences; veiled hints that revealed in half concealing. Her husband's friend Richards was there, too, near her. It was he who had been in the newspaper office when intelligence of the railroad disaster was received, with Brently Mallard's name leading the list of "killed." He had only taken the time to assure himself of its truth by a second telegram, and had hastened to forestall any less careful, less tender friend in bearing the sad message.

She did not hear the story as many women have heard the same, with a paralyzed inability to accept its significance. She wept at once, with sudden, wild abandonment, in her sister's arms. When the storm of grief had spent itself she went away to her room alone. She would have no one follow her.

There stood, facing the open window, a comfortable, roomy armchair. Into this she sank, pressed down by a physical exhaustion that haunted her body and seemed to reach into her soul.

Excerpt from "The Story of an Hour" by Kate Chopin

Now, using the outline above, the similarities and differences between the three passages are considered:

1. **Style:** Passage I is an expository style, presenting purely factual evidence on death, completely devoid of emotion. Passage II is a narrative style, where the theme of death is presented to us by the reaction of the loved ones involved. This narrative style is full of emotional language and imagery.

2. **Tone:** Passage I has no emotionally-charged words of any kind, and seems to view death simply as a process that happens, neither welcoming nor fearing it. The tone in this passage, therefore, is neutral. Passage II does not have a neutral tone—it uses words like "disaster," "killed," "sad," "wept," "wild abandonment," and "physical exhaustion," implying an anxiety toward the theme of death.

3. **Sentence Structure:** Passage I contains many complex-compound sentences, which are used to accommodate lots of information. The structure of these sentences contributes to the overall informative nature of the selection. Passage II has several compound sentences and complex sentences on their own. It's also marked by the use of many commas in a single sentence, separating modifying words. Perhaps this variety is meant to match the sporadic emotion of the character's discovery of her husband's death.

4. **Punctuation Choice:** Passage I uses only commas and periods, which adds to the overall neutral tone of the selection. Passage II mostly uses commas and periods, and then one semicolon. Again, the excess of commas and semicolon in the first sentence may be said to mirror the character's anxiety.

5. **Point of View:** Passage I uses third-person point of view, as it avoids any first- or second-person pronouns. Passage II also uses third-person point of view, as the story is being told by a narrator about characters separate from the narrator.

6. **Paragraph Structure:** The first passage is told in an objective way, and each paragraph is focused on the topic brought up in the first sentence. The second passage has no specific topic per paragraph. It is organized in a sequential way, so the paragraphs flow into the next in a chronological order.

7. **Organizational Structure:** The structure of Passage I is told in a very objective, organized way. The first paragraph tells of the stages before death, and the second paragraph tells of the stages after death. The second passage is told in chronological order, as a sequence of events, like in a fictional story.

When analyzing the different structures, it may be helpful to make a table and use single words to compare and contrast the texts:

Elements	**Passage I**	**Passage II**
Style	Expository	Narrative
Tone	Neutral	Emotional
Sentence Structure	Long	Long/Sporadic
Punctuation Choice	.	. and ,
Point of View	Third	Third
Paragraph Structure	Focused	Sequential
Organizational Structure	Objective/Logical	Chronological

The main differences between the two selections are style, tone, and structure. Possibly the most noticeable difference is the style and tone, as one tone is more neutral, and the other tone is more emotional. This is due to the word choice used and how each passage treats the topic of death. These are only a handful of the endless possible interpretations the reader could make.

Analyzing How Authors Construct Arguments

<u>Constructing Arguments Through Evidence</u>

Using only one form of supporting evidence is not nearly as effective as using a variety to support a claim. Presenting only a list of statistics can be boring to the reader but providing a true story that's both interesting and humanizing helps. In addition, one example isn't always enough to prove the writer's larger point, so combining it with other examples in the writing is extremely effective. Thus, when reading a passage, readers should not just look for a single form of supporting evidence.

For example, although most people can't argue with the statement, "Seat belts save lives", its impact on the reader is much greater when supported by additional content. The writer can support this idea by:

- Providing statistics on the rate of highway fatalities alongside statistics of estimated seat belt usage.
- Explaining the science behind car accidents and what happens to a passenger who doesn't use a seat belt.
- Offering anecdotal evidence or true stories from reliable sources on how seat belts prevent fatal injuries in car crashes.

Another key aspect of supporting evidence is a **reliable source**. Does the writer include the source of the information? If so, is the source well-known and trustworthy? Is there a potential for bias? For example, a seat belt study done by a seat belt manufacturer may have its own agenda to promote.

Logical Sequence

Even if the writer includes plenty of information to support his or her point, the writing is only effective when the information is in a logical order. **Logical sequencing** is really just common sense, but it's an important writing technique. First, the writer should introduce the main idea, whether for a paragraph, a section, or the entire text. Then he or she should present evidence to support the main idea by using transitional language. This shows the reader how the information relates to the main idea and to the sentences around it. The writer should then take time to interpret the information, making sure necessary connections are obvious to the reader. Finally, the writer can summarize the information in the closing section.

NOTE: Although most writing follows this pattern, it isn't a set rule. Sometimes writers change the order for effect. For example, the writer can begin with a surprising piece of supporting information to grab the reader's attention, and then transition to the main idea. Thus, if a passage doesn't follow the logical order, readers should not immediately assume it's wrong. However, most writing that has a nontraditional beginning usually settles into a logical sequence.

Sentence Skills

Sentence Correction

In this section of the test, each example contains a sentence with an underlined portion. The multiple choice answers will offer reworded versions of the underlined part of the sentence. The first answer choice will repeat the original sentence, and the others will offer different options for how to re-word the sentence.

The goal of these questions is to test an individual's ability to recognize the most effective way to express something, using correct grammar, word choice, and sentence structure. The correct answer will be grammatically-correct, with a clear, concise flow.

Construction Shift

These multiple-choice questions ask the test-taker to rewrite the original sentence so that it is more correct in terms of grammar, word choice, and sentence structure. These questions will provide the beginning of the new sentence and then offer four options for ending the sentence. The goal is to select the answer choice that makes the best structured sentence, while retaining the meaning of the original sentence. In most cases, when the sentence is rewritten, it will entail changing a dependent clause to an independent clause, or an independent clause to a dependent clause.

Answers should be chosen carefully, ensuring that they adhere to the rules of grammar and standard English. The best choice will be the one that is correct, concise, and clear, while also retaining the meaning of the original sentence.

A helpful strategy is to predict the sentence ending before looking at the answer choices. This approach helps in selecting the one that makes the most sense. Reading the answer choices first might be confusing and make the choice more difficult. In these questions, the simplest answer is often the best answer.

Types of Sentences

There isn't an overabundance of absolutes in grammar, but here is one: every sentence in the English language falls into one of four categories.

- Declarative: a simple statement that ends with a period

  The price of milk per gallon is the same as the price of gasoline.

- Imperative: a command, instruction, or request that ends with a period

  Buy milk when you stop to fill up your car with gas.

- Interrogative: a question that ends with a question mark

  Will you buy the milk?

- Exclamatory: a statement or command that expresses emotions like anger, urgency, or surprise and ends with an exclamation mark

  Buy the milk now!

Declarative sentences are the most common type, probably because they are comprised of the most general content, without any of the bells and whistles that the other three types contain. They are, simply, declarations or statements of any degree of seriousness, importance, or information.

Imperative sentences often seem to be missing a subject. The subject is there, though; it is just not visible or audible because it is *implied.* Look at the imperative example sentence.

Buy the milk when you fill up your car with gas.

You is the implied subject, the one to whom the command is issued. This is sometimes called *the understood you* because it is understood that *you* is the subject of the sentence.

Interrogative sentences—those that ask questions—are defined as such from the idea of the word *interrogation*, the action of questions being asked of suspects by investigators. Although that is serious business, interrogative sentences apply to all kinds of questions.

To exclaim is at the root of *exclamatory* sentences. These are made with strong emotions behind them. The only technical difference between a declarative or imperative sentence and an exclamatory one is the exclamation mark at the end. The example declarative and imperative sentences can both become an exclamatory one simply by putting an exclamation mark at the end of the sentences.

The price of milk per gallon is the same as the price of gasoline!
Buy milk when you stop to fill up your car with gas!

After all, someone might be really excited by the price of gas or milk, or they could be mad at the person that will be buying the milk! However, as stated before, exclamation marks in abundance defeat their own purpose! After a while, they begin to cause fatigue! When used only for their intended purpose, they can have their expected and desired effect.

Parts of Speech

<u>Nouns</u>
A noun is a person, place, thing, or idea. All nouns fit into one of two types, common or proper.

A *common noun* is a word that identifies any of a class of people, places, or things. Examples include numbers, objects, animals, feelings, concepts, qualities, and actions. *A, an,* or *the* usually precedes the common noun. These parts of speech are called *articles*. Here are some examples of sentences using nouns preceded by articles.

A building is under construction.
The girl would like to move to *the* city.

A *proper noun* (also called a *proper name*) is used for the specific name of an individual person, place, or organization. The first letter in a proper noun is capitalized. "My name is *Mary*." "I work for *Walmart*."

Nouns sometimes serve as adjectives (which themselves describe nouns), such as "hockey player" and "state government."

An abstract noun is an idea, state, or quality. It is something that can't be touched, such as happiness, courage, evil, or humor.

A concrete noun is something that can be experienced through the senses (touch, taste, hear, smell, see). Examples of concrete nouns are birds, skateboard, pie, and car.

A collective noun refers to a collection of people, places, or things that act as one. Examples of collective nouns are as follows: team, class, jury, family, audience, and flock.

<u>Pronouns</u>
A word used in place of a noun is known as a *pronoun*. Pronouns are words like *I, mine, hers,* and *us*.

Pronouns can be split into different classifications (see below) which make them easier to learn; however, it's not important to memorize the classifications.

- Personal pronouns: refer to people
- First person: we, I, our, mine
- Second person: you, yours
- Third person: he, them
- Possessive pronouns: demonstrate ownership (mine, my, his, yours)
- Interrogative pronouns: ask questions (what, which, who, whom, whose)
- Relative pronouns: include the five interrogative pronouns and others that are relative (whoever, whomever, that, when, where)
- Demonstrative pronouns: replace something specific (this, that, those, these)
- Reciprocal pronouns: indicate something was done or given in return (each other, one another)
- Indefinite pronouns: have a nonspecific status (anybody, whoever, someone, everybody, somebody)

Indefinite pronouns such as *anybody, whoever, someone, everybody*, and *somebody* command a singular verb form, but others such as *all, none,* and *some* could require a singular or plural verb form.

<u>Antecedents</u>
An *antecedent* is the noun to which a pronoun refers; it needs to be written or spoken before the pronoun is used. For many pronouns, antecedents are imperative for clarity. In particular, many of the personal, possessive, and demonstrative pronouns need antecedents. Otherwise, it would be unclear who or what someone is referring to when they use a pronoun like *he* or *this*.

Pronoun reference means that the pronoun should refer clearly to one, clear, unmistakable noun (the antecedent).

Pronoun-antecedent agreement refers to the need for the antecedent and the corresponding pronoun to agree in gender, person, and number. Here are some examples:

> The *kidneys* (plural antecedent) are part of the urinary system. *They* (plural pronoun) serve several roles."
>
> The kidneys are part of the *urinary system* (singular antecedent). *It* (singular pronoun) is also known as the renal system.

<u>Pronoun Cases</u>
The subjective pronouns —*I, you, he/she/it, we, they,* and *who*—are the subjects of the sentence.

> Example: *They* have a new house.

The objective pronouns—*me, you* (*singular*), *him/her, us, them,* and *whom*—are used when something is being done for or given to someone; they are objects of the action.

> Example: The teacher has an apple for *us*.

The possessive pronouns—*mine, my, your, yours, his, hers, its, their, theirs, our,* and *ours*—are used to denote that something (or someone) belongs to someone (or something).

> Example: It's *their* chocolate cake.
> Even Better Example: It's *my* chocolate cake!

One of the greatest challenges and worst abuses of pronouns concerns *who* and *whom*. Just knowing the following rule can eliminate confusion. *Who* is a subjective-case pronoun used only as a subject or subject complement. *Whom* is only objective-case and, therefore, the object of the verb or preposition.

> *Who* is going to the concert?
>
> You are going to the concert with *whom*?

Hint: When using *who* or *whom*, think of whether someone would say *he* or *him*. If the answer is *he*, use *who*. If the answer is *him*, use *whom*. This trick is easy to remember because *he* and *who* both end in vowels, and *him* and *whom* both end in the letter *M*.

<u>Verbs</u>
The *verb* is the part of speech that describes an action, state of being, or occurrence.

A *verb* forms the main part of a predicate of a sentence. This means that the verb explains what the noun (which will be discussed shortly) is doing. A simple example is *time <u>flies</u>*. The verb *flies* explains what the action of the noun, *time*, is doing. This example is a *main* verb.

Helping (*auxiliary*) verbs are words like *have, do, be, can, may, should, must,* and *will.* "I *should* go to the store." Helping verbs assist main verbs in expressing tense, ability, possibility, permission, or obligation.

Particles are minor function words like *not, in, out, up,* or *down* that become part of the verb itself. "I might *not*."

Participles are words formed from verbs that are often used to modify a noun, noun phrase, verb, or verb phrase.

> The *running* teenager collided with the cyclist.

Participles can also create compound verb forms.

> He is *speaking*.

Verbs have five basic forms: the *base* form, the *-s* form, the *-ing* form, the *past* form, and the *past participle* form.

The *past* forms are either *regular* (*love/loved; hate/hated*) or *irregular* because they don't end by adding the common past tense suffix "-ed" (*go/went; fall/fell; set/set*).

<u>Verb Forms</u>
Shifting verb forms entails *conjugation*, which is used to indicate *tense, voice,* or *mood.*

Verb tense is used to show when the action in the sentence took place. There are several different verb tenses, and it is important to know how and when to use them. Some verb tenses can be achieved by changing the form of the verb, while others require the use of helping verbs (e.g., *is, was,* or *has*).

Present tense shows the action is happening currently or is ongoing:

> I walk to work every morning.
>
> She is stressed about the deadline.

Past tense shows that the action happened in the past or that the state of being is in the past:

> I walked to work yesterday morning.
>
> She was stressed about the deadline.

Future tense shows that the action will happen in the future or is a future state of being:

> I will walk to work tomorrow morning.
>
> She will be stressed about the deadline.

Present perfect tense shows action that began in the past, but continues into the present:

> I have walked to work all week.
>
> She has been stressed about the deadline.

Past perfect tense shows an action was finished before another took place:

> I had walked all week until I sprained my ankle.
>
> She had been stressed about the deadline until we talked about it.

Future perfect tense shows an action that will be completed at some point in the future:

By the time the bus arrives, I will have walked to work already.

Voice

Verbs can be in the active or passive voice. When the subject completes the action, the verb is in *active voice*. When the subject receives the action of the sentence, the verb is in *passive voice*.

Active: Jamie ate the ice cream.

Passive: The ice cream was eaten by Jamie.

In active voice, the subject (*Jamie*) is the "do-er" of the action (*ate*). In passive voice, the subject *ice cream* receives the action of being eaten.

While passive voice can add variety to writing, active voice is the generally preferred sentence structure.

Mood

Mood is used to show the speaker's feelings about the subject matter. In English, there is *indicative mood, imperative mood,* and *subjective mood.*

Indicative mood is used to state facts, ask questions, or state opinions:

Bob will make the trip next week.

When can Bob make the trip?

Imperative mood is used to state a command or make a request:

Wait in the lobby.

Please call me next week.

Subjunctive mood is used to express a wish, an opinion, or a hope that is contrary to fact:

If I were in charge, none of this would have happened.

Allison wished she could take the exam over again when she saw her score.

Adjectives

Adjectives are words used to modify nouns and pronouns. They can be used alone or in a series and are used to further define or describe the nouns they modify.

Mark made us a delicious, four-course meal.

The words *delicious* and *four-course* are adjectives that describe the kind of meal Mark made.

Articles are also considered adjectives because they help to describe nouns. Articles can be general or specific. The three articles in English are: a, an, and the.

Indefinite articles (a, an) are used to refer to nonspecific nouns. The article *a* proceeds words beginning with consonant sounds, and the article *an* proceeds words beginning with vowel sounds.

A car drove by our house.

An alligator was loose at the zoo.

He has always wanted a ukulele. (The first *u* makes a *y* sound.)

Note that *a* and *an* should only proceed nonspecific nouns that are also singular. If a nonspecific noun is plural, it does not need a preceding article.

Alligators were loose at the zoo.

The *definite article (the)* is used to refer to specific nouns:

The car pulled into our driveway.

Note that *the* should proceed all specific nouns regardless of whether they are singular or plural.

The cars pulled into our driveway.

Comparative adjectives are used to compare nouns. When they are used in this way, they take on positive, comparative, or superlative form.

The *positive* form is the normal form of the adjective:

Alicia is tall.

The *comparative* form shows a comparison between two things:

Alicia is taller than Maria.

Superlative form shows comparison between more than two things:

Alicia is the tallest girl in her class.

Usually, the comparative and superlative can be made by adding *–er* and *–est* to the positive form, but some verbs call for the helping verbs *more* or *most*. Other exceptions to the rule include adjectives like *bad*, which uses the comparative *worse* and the superlative *worst*.

An adjective phrase is not a bunch of adjectives strung together, but a group of words that describes a noun or pronoun and, thus, functions as an adjective. *Very ugly* is an adjective phrase; so are *way too fat* and *faster than a speeding bullet.*

<u>Adverbs</u>

Adverbs have more functions than adjectives because they modify or qualify verbs, adjectives, or other adverbs as well as word groups that express a relation of place, time, circumstance, or cause. Therefore, adverbs answer any of the following questions: *How, when, where, why, in what way, how often, how much, in what condition,* and/or *to what degree. How good looking is he? He is <u>very</u> handsome.*

Here are some examples of adverbs for different situations:

- how: quickly
- when: daily
- where: there
- in what way: easily
- how often: often
- how much: much
- in what condition: badly
- what degree: hardly

As one can see, for some reason, many adverbs end in *-ly.*

Adverbs do things like emphasize (*really, simply,* and *so*), amplify (*heartily, completely,* and *positively*), and tone down (*almost, somewhat,* and *mildly*).

Adverbs also come in phrases.

The dog ran as <u>though his life depended on it.</u>

<u>Prepositions</u>

Prepositions are connecting words and, while there are only about 150 of them, they are used more often than any other individual groups of words. They describe relationships between other words. They are placed before a noun or pronoun, forming a phrase that modifies another word in the sentence. *Prepositional phrases* begin with a preposition and end with a noun or pronoun, the *object of the preposition. A pristine lake is <u>near the store</u> and <u>behind the bank</u>.*

Some commonly used prepositions are *about, after, anti, around, as, at, behind, beside, by, for, from, in, into, of, off, on, to,* and *with.*

Complex prepositions, which also come before a noun or pronoun, consist of two or three words such as *according to, in regards to,* and *because of.*

<u>Conjunctions</u>

Conjunctions are vital words that connect words, phrases, thoughts, and ideas. Conjunctions show relationships between components. There are two types:

Coordinating conjunctions are the primary class of conjunctions placed between words, phrases, clauses, and sentences that are of equal grammatical rank; the coordinating conjunctions are for, and, nor, but, or, yes, and so. A useful memorization trick is to remember that all the first letters of these conjunctions collectively spell the word fanboys.

I need to go shopping, *but* I must be careful to leave enough money in the bank.
She wore a black, red, *and* white shirt.

Subordinating conjunctions are the secondary class of conjunctions. They connect two unequal parts, one *main* (or *independent*) and the other *subordinate* (or *dependent*). I must go to the store *even though* I do not have enough money in the bank.

Because I read the review, I do not want to go to the movie.

Notice that the presence of subordinating conjunctions makes clauses dependent. *I read the review* is an independent clause, but *because* makes the clause dependent. Thus, it needs an independent clause to complete the sentence.

Interjections

Interjections are words used to express emotion. Examples include *wow*, *ouch*, and *hooray*. Interjections are often separate from sentences; in those cases, the interjection is directly followed by an exclamation point. In other cases, the interjection is included in a sentence and followed by a comma. The punctuation plays a big role in the intensity of the emotion that the interjection is expressing. Using a comma or semicolon indicates less excitement than using an exclamation mark.

Capitalization Rules

Here's a non-exhaustive list of things that should be capitalized.

- The first word of every sentence
- The first word of every line of poetry
- The first letter of proper nouns (World War II)
- Holidays (Valentine's Day)
- The days of the week and months of the year (Tuesday, March)
- The first word, last word, and all major words in the titles of books, movies, songs, and other creative works (In the novel, *To Kill a Mockingbird*, note that *a* is lowercase since it's not a major word, but *to* is capitalized since it's the first word of the title.)
- Titles when preceding a proper noun (President Roberto Gonzales, Aunt Judy)

When simply using a word such as president or secretary, though, the word is not capitalized.

Officers of the new business must include a *president* and *treasurer*.

Seasons—spring, fall, etc.—are not capitalized.

North, *south*, *east*, and *west* are capitalized when referring to regions but are not when being used for directions. In general, if it's preceded by *the* it should be capitalized.

I'm from the South.
I drove south.

End Punctuation

Periods (.) are used to end a sentence that is a statement (*declarative*) or a command (*imperative*). They should not be used in a sentence that asks a question or is an exclamation. Periods are also used in abbreviations, which are shortened versions of words.

- Declarative: The boys refused to go to sleep.
- Imperative: Walk down to the bus stop.
- Abbreviations: Joan Roberts, M.D., Apple Inc., Mrs. Adamson
- If a sentence ends with an abbreviation, it is inappropriate to use two periods. It should end with a single period after the abbreviation.

The chef gathered the ingredients for the pie, which included apples, flour, sugar, etc.

Question marks (?) are used with direct questions (*interrogative*). An *indirect question* can use a period:

Interrogative: When does the next bus arrive?

Indirect Question: I wonder when the next bus arrives.

An *exclamation point (!)* is used to show strong emotion or can be used as an *interjection*. This punctuation should be used sparingly in formal writing situations.

What an amazing shot!

Whoa!

Commas

A *comma* (,) is the punctuation mark that signifies a pause—breath—between parts of a sentence. It denotes a break of flow. Proper comma usage helps readers understand the writer's intended emphasis of ideas.

In a complex sentence—one that contains a subordinate (dependent) clause or clauses—the use of a comma is dictated by where the subordinate clause is located. If the subordinate clause is located before the main clause, a comma is needed between the two clauses.

I will not pay for the steak, *because I don't have that much money.*

Generally, if the subordinate clause is placed after the main clause, no punctuation is needed. I did well on my exam because I studied two hours the night before. Notice how the last clause is dependent because it requires the earlier independent clauses to make sense.

Use a comma on both sides of an interrupting phrase.

I will pay for the ice cream, chocolate and vanilla, and then will eat it all myself.

The words forming the phrase in italics are nonessential (extra) information. To determine if a phrase is nonessential, try reading the sentence without the phrase and see if it's still coherent.

A comma is not necessary in this next sentence because no interruption—nonessential or extra information—has occurred. Read sentences aloud when uncertain.

I will pay for his chocolate and vanilla ice cream and then will eat it all myself.

If the nonessential phrase comes at the beginning of a sentence, a comma should only go at the end of the phrase. If the phrase comes at the end of a sentence, a comma should only go at the beginning of the phrase.

Other types of interruptions include the following:

- interjections: Oh no, I am not going.
- abbreviations: Barry Potter, M.D., specializes in heart disorders.
- direct addresses: Yes, Claudia, I am tired and going to bed.
- parenthetical phrases: His wife, lovely as she was, was not helpful.
- transitional phrases: Also, it is not possible.

The second comma in the following sentence is called an Oxford comma.

> I will pay for ice cream, syrup, and pop.

It is a comma used after the second-to-last item in a series of three or more items. It comes before the word *or* or *and*. Not everyone uses the Oxford comma; it is optional, but many believe it is needed. The comma functions as a tool to reduce confusion in writing. So, if omitting the Oxford comma would cause confusion, then it's best to include it.

Commas are used in math to mark the place of thousands in numerals, breaking them up so they are easier to read. Other uses for commas are in dates (*March 19, 2016*), letter greetings (*Dear Sally,*), and in between cities and states (*Louisville, KY*).

Semicolons

A *semicolon (;)* is used to connect ideas in a sentence in some way. There are three main ways to use semicolons.

Link two independent clauses without the use of a coordinating conjunction:

> I was late for work again; I'm definitely going to get fired.

Link two independent clauses with a transitional word:

> The songs were all easy to play; therefore, he didn't need to spend too much time practicing.

Between items in a series that are already separated by commas or if necessary to separate lengthy items in a list:

> Starbucks has locations in Media, PA; Swarthmore, PA; and Morton, PA.
>
> Several classroom management issues presented in the study: the advent of a poor teacher persona in the context of voice, dress, and style; teacher follow-through from the beginning of the school year to the end; and the depth of administrative support, including ISS and OSS protocol.

Colons

A *colon* is used after an independent clause to present an explanation or draw attention to what comes next in the sentence. There are several uses.

Explanations of ideas:

> They soon learned the hardest part about having a new baby: sleep deprivation.

Lists of items:

> Shari picked up all the supplies she would need for the party: cups, plates, napkins, balloons, streamers, and party favors.

Time, subtitles, general salutations:

The time is 7:15.

I read a book entitled *Pluto: A Planet No More*.

To whom it may concern:

Parentheses and Dashes

Parentheses are half-round brackets that look like this: *( )*. They set off a word, phrase, or sentence that is an afterthought, explanation, or side note relevant to the surrounding text but not essential. A pair of commas is often used to set off this sort of information, but parentheses are generally used for information that would not fit well within a sentence or that the writer deems not important enough to be structurally part of the sentence.

The picture of the heart (see above) shows the major parts you should memorize.
Mount Everest is one of three mountains in the world that are over 28,000 feet high (K2 and Kanchenjunga are the other two).

See how the sentences above are complete without the parenthetical statements? In the first example, *see above* would not have fit well within the flow of the sentence. The second parenthetical statement could have been a separate sentence, but the writer deemed the information not pertinent to the topic.

The dash (—) is a mark longer than a hyphen used as a punctuation mark in sentences and to set apart a relevant thought. Even after plucking out the line separated by the dash marks, the sentence will be intact and make sense.

Looking out the airplane window at the landmarks—Lake Clarke, Thompson Community College, and the bridge—she couldn't help but feel excited to be home.

The dashes use is similar to that of parentheses or a pair of commas. So, what's the difference? Many believe that using dashes makes the clause within them stand out while using parentheses is subtler. It's advised to not use dashes when commas could be used instead.

Ellipses

An *ellipsis* (...) consists of three handy little dots that can speak volumes on behalf of irrelevant material. Writers use them in place of words, lines, phrases, list content, or paragraphs that might just as easily have been omitted from a passage of writing. This can be done to save space or to focus only on the specifically relevant material.

Exercise is good for some unexpected reasons. Watkins writes, "Exercise has many benefits such as...reducing cancer risk."

In the example above, the ellipsis takes the place of the other benefits of exercise that are more expected.

The ellipsis may also be used to show a pause in sentence flow.

"I'm wondering...how this could happen," Dylan said in a soft voice.

Quotation Marks

Double *quotation marks* are used to at the beginning and end of a direct quote. They are also used with certain titles and to indicate that a term being used is slang or referenced in the sentence. Quotation marks should not be used with an indirect quote. Single quotation marks are used to indicate a quote within a quote.

Direct quote: "The weather is supposed to be beautiful this week," she said.

Indirect quote: One of the customers asked if the sale prices were still in effect.

Quote within a quote: "My little boy just said 'Mama, I want cookie,'" Maria shared.

Titles: Quotation marks should also be used to indicate titles of short works or sections of larger works, such as chapter titles. Other works that use quotation marks include poems, short stories, newspaper articles, magazine articles, web page titles, and songs.

"The Road Not Taken" is my favorite poem by Robert Frost.

"What a Wonderful World" is one of my favorite songs.

Specific or emphasized terms: Quotation marks can also be used to indicate a technical term or to set off a word that is being discussed in a sentence. Quotation marks can also indicate sarcasm.

The new step, called "levigation", is a very difficult technique.

He said he was "hungry" multiple times, but he only ate two bites.

Use with other punctuation: The use of quotation marks with other punctuation varies, depending on the role of the ending or separating punctuation.

In American English, *periods* and *commas* always go inside the quotation marks:

"This is the last time you are allowed to leave early," his boss stated.

The newscaster said, "We have some breaking news to report."

Question marks or *exclamation points* go inside the quotation marks when they are part of a direct quote:

The doctor shouted, "Get the crash cart!"

When the question mark or exclamation point is part of the sentence, not the quote, it should be placed outside of the quotation marks:

Was it Jackie that said, "Get some potatoes at the store"?

Apostrophes

This punctuation mark, the apostrophe (') is a versatile mark. It has several different functions:

- Quotes: Apostrophes are used when a second quote is needed within a quote.

  In my letter to my friend, I wrote, "The girl had to get a new purse, and guess what Mary did? She said, 'I'd like to go with you to the store.' I knew Mary would buy it for her."

- Contractions: Another use for an apostrophe in the quote above is a contraction. *I'd* is used for *I would.*

- Possession: An apostrophe followed by the letter s shows possession (Mary's purse). If the possessive word is plural, the apostrophe generally just follows the word. Not all possessive pronouns require apostrophes.

  The trees' leaves are all over the ground.

Hyphens

The *hyphen* (-) is a small hash mark that can be used to join words to show that they are linked.

Hyphenate two words that work together as a single adjective (a compound adjective).

honey-covered biscuits

Some words always require hyphens, even if not serving as an adjective.

merry-go-round

Hyphens always go after certain prefixes like *anti-* & *all-*.

Hyphens should also be used when the absence of the hyphen would cause a strange vowel combination (*semi-engineer*) or confusion. For example, *re-collect* should be used to describe something being gathered twice rather than being written as *recollect*, which means to remember.

Subjects

Every sentence must include a subject and a verb. The *subject* of a sentence is who or what the sentence is about. It's often directly stated and can be determined by asking "Who?" or "What?" did the action:

Most sentences contain a direct subject, in which the subject is mentioned in the sentence.

Kelly mowed the lawn.

Who mowed the lawn? *Kelly*

The air-conditioner ran all night

What ran all night? *the air-conditioner*

The subject of imperative sentences is *you*, because imperative subjects are commands. the subject is implied because it is a command:

Go home after the meeting.

Who should go home after the meeting? *you* (implied)

In *expletive sentences* that start with "there are" or "there is," the subject is found after the predicate. The subject cannot be "there," so it must be another word in the sentence:

There is a cup sitting on the coffee table.

What is sitting on the coffee table? *a cup*

Simple and Complete Subjects

A *complete subject* includes the simple subject and all the words modifying it, including articles and adjectives. A *simple subject* is the single noun without its modifiers.

A warm, chocolate-chip cookie sat on the kitchen table.

Complete subject: *a warm, chocolate-chip cookie*

Simple subject: *cookie*

The words *a, warm, chocolate,* and *chip* all modify the simple subject *cookie.*

There might also be a *compound subject*, which would be two or more nouns without the modifiers.

A little girl and her mother walked into the shop.

Complete subject: *A little girl and her mother*

Compound subject: *girl, mother*

In this case, *the girl and her mother* are both completing the action of walking into the shop, so this is a *compound subject*.

Predicates

In addition to the subject, a sentence must also have a predicate. The *predicate* contains a verb and tells something about the subject. In addition to the verb, a predicate can also contain a direct or indirect object, object of a preposition, and other phrases.

The cats napped on the front porch.

In this sentence, cats is the subject because the sentence is about cats.

The *complete predicate* is everything else in the sentence: *napped on the front porch.* This phrase is the predicate because it tells us what the cats did.

This sentence can be broken down into a simple subject and predicate:

Cats napped.

In this sentence, *cats* is the simple subject, and *napped* is the *simple predicate*.

Although the sentence is very short and doesn't offer much information, it's still considered a complete sentence because it contains a subject and predicate.

Like a compound subject, a sentence can also have a ***compound predicate***. This is when the subject is or does two or more things in the sentence.

This easy chair reclines and swivels.

In this sentence, *this easy chair* is the complete subject. *Reclines and swivels* shows two actions of the chair, so this is the compound predicate.

Subject-Verb Agreement

The subject of a sentence and its verb must agree. The cornerstone rule of subject-verb agreement is that subject and verb must agree in number. Whether the subject is singular or plural, the verb must follow suit.

Incorrect: The houses is new.
Correct: The houses are new.
Also Correct: The house is new.

In other words, a singular subject requires a singular verb; a plural subject requires a plural verb. The words or phrases that come between the subject and verb do not alter this rule.

Incorrect: The houses built of brick is new.
Correct: The houses built of brick are new.

Incorrect: The houses with the sturdy porches is new.
Correct: The houses with the sturdy porches are new.

The subject will always follow the verb when a sentence begins with *here* or *there.* Identify these with care.

Incorrect: Here *is* the *houses* with sturdy porches.
Correct: Here *are* the *houses* with sturdy porches.

The subject in the sentences above is not *here*, it is *houses*. Remember, *here* and *there* are never subjects. Be careful that contractions such as *here's* or *there're* do not cause confusion!

Two subjects joined by *and* require a plural verb form, except when the two combine to make one thing:

Incorrect: Garrett and Jonathan is over there.
Correct: Garrett and Jonathan are over there.

Incorrect: Spaghetti and meatballs are a delicious meal!
Correct: Spaghetti and meatballs is a delicious meal!

In the example above, *spaghetti and meatballs* is a compound noun. However, *Garrett and Jonathan* is not a compound noun.

Two singular subjects joined by *or, either/or,* or *neither/nor* call for a singular verb form.

> Incorrect: Butter or syrup are acceptable.
> Correct: Butter or syrup is acceptable.

Plural subjects joined by *or, either/or,* or *neither/nor* are, indeed, plural.

> The chairs or the boxes are being moved next.

If one subject is singular and the other is plural, the verb should agree with the closest noun.

> Correct: The chair or the boxes are being moved next.
> Correct: The chairs or the box is being moved next.

Some plurals of money, distance, and time call for a singular verb.

> Incorrect: Three dollars *are* enough to buy that.
> Correct: Three dollars *is* enough to buy that.

For words declaring degrees of quantity such as *many of, some of,* or *most of,* let the noun that follows of be the guide:

> Incorrect: Many of the books is in the shelf.
> Correct: Many of the books are in the shelf.

> Incorrect: Most of the pie *are* on the table.
> Correct: Most of the pie *is* on the table.

For indefinite pronouns like anybody or everybody, use singular verbs.

> Everybody *is* going to the store.

However, the pronouns *few, many, several, all, some,* and *both* have their own rules and use plural forms.

> Some *are* ready.

Some nouns like *crowd* and *congress* are called *collective nouns* and they require a singular verb form.

> Congress *is* in session.
> The news *is* over.

Books and movie titles, though, including plural nouns such as *Great Expectations*, also require a singular verb. Remember that only the subject affects the verb. While writing tricky subject-verb arrangements, say them aloud. Listen to them. Once the rules have been learned, one's ear will become sensitive to them, making it easier to pick out what's right and what's wrong.

Direct Objects

The *direct object* is the part of the sentence that receives the action of the verb. It is a noun and can usually be found after the verb. To find the direct object, first find the verb, and then ask the question *who* or *what* after it.

The bear climbed the tree.

What did the bear climb? *the tree*

Indirect Objects

An *indirect object* receives the direct object. It is usually found between the verb and the direct object. A strategy for identifying the indirect object is to find the verb and ask the questions *to whom/for whom* or *to what/ for what.*

Jane made her daughter a cake.

For whom did Jane make the cake? *her daughter*

Cake is the direct object because it is what Jane made, and *daughter* is the indirect object because she receives the cake.

Complements

A *complement* completes the meaning of an expression. A complement can be a pronoun, noun, or adjective. A verb complement refers to the direct object or indirect object in the sentence. An object complement gives more information about the direct object:

The magician got the kids excited.

Kids is the direct object, and *excited* is the object complement.

A *subject complement* comes after a linking verb. It is typically an adjective or noun that gives more information about the subject:

The king was noble and spared the thief's life.

Noble describes the *king* and follows the linking verb *was.*

Predicate Nouns

A *predicate noun* renames the subject:

John is a carpenter.

The subject is *John*, and the predicate noun is *carpenter.*

Predicate Adjectives

A *predicate adjective* describes the subject:

Margaret is beautiful.

The subject is *Margaret*, and the predicate adjective is *beautiful*.

Homonyms

Homonyms are words that sound the same but are spelled differently, and they have different meanings. There are several common homonyms that give writers trouble.

There, They're, and *Their*

The word *there* can be used as an adverb, adjective, or pronoun:

There are ten children on the swim team this summer.

I put my book over *there*, but now I can't find it.

The word *they're* is a contraction of the words *they* and *are*:

They're flying in from Texas on Tuesday.

The word *their* is a possessive pronoun:

I store *their* winter clothes in the attic.

Its and *It's*

Its is a possessive pronoun:

The cat licked *its* injured paw.

It's is the contraction for the words *it* and *is*:

It's unbelievable how many people opted not to vote in the last election.

Your and You're

Your is a possessive pronoun:

Can I borrow *your* lawnmower this weekend?

You're is a contraction for the words *you* and *are*:

You're about to embark on a fantastic journey.

To, Too, and *Two*

To is an adverb or a preposition used to show direction, relationship, or purpose:

We are going *to* New York.

They are going *to* see a show.

Too is an adverb that means more than enough, also, and very:

You have had *too* much candy.

We are on vacation that week, *too*.

Two is the written-out form of the numeral 2:

Two of the shirts didn't fit, so I will have to return them.

<u>*New* and *Knew*</u>
New is an adjective that means recent:

There's a *new* customer on the phone.

Knew is the past tense of the verb *know*:

I *knew* you'd have fun on this ride.

<u>*Affect* and *Effect*</u>
Affect and *effect* are complicated because they are used as both nouns and verbs, have similar meanings, and are pronounced the same.

	Affect	**Effect**
Noun Definition	emotional state	result
Noun Example	The patient's affect was flat.	The effects of smoking are well documented.
Verb Definition	to influence	to bring about
Verb Example	The pollen count affects my allergies.	The new candidate hopes to effect change.

Independent and Dependent Clauses

Independent and *dependent* clauses are strings of words that contain both a subject and a verb. An independent clause *can* stand alone as complete thought, but a dependent clause *cannot*. A dependent clause relies on other words to be a complete sentence.

Independent clause: The keys are on the counter.
Dependent clause: If the keys are on the counter

Notice that both clauses have a subject (*keys*) and a verb (*are*). The independent clause expresses a complete thought, but the word *if* at the beginning of the dependent clause makes it *dependent* on other words to be a complete thought.

Independent clause: If the keys are on the counter, please give them to me.

This presents a complete sentence since it includes at least one verb and one subject and is a complete thought. In this case, the independent clause has two subjects (*keys* & an implied *you*) and two verbs (*are* & *give*).

Independent clause: I went to the store.
Dependent clause: Because we are out of milk,

Complete Sentence: Because we are out of milk, I went to the store.
Complete Sentence: I went to the store because we are out of milk.

Phrases

A *phrase* is a group of words that do not make a complete thought or a clause. They are parts of sentences or clauses. Phrases can be used as nouns, adjectives, or adverbs. A phrase does not contain both a subject and a verb.

Prepositional Phrases

A *prepositional phrase* shows the relationship between a word in the sentence and the object of the preposition. The object of the preposition is a noun that follows the preposition.

The orange pillows are on the couch.

On is the preposition, and *couch* is the object of the preposition.

She brought her friend with the nice car.

With is the preposition, and *car* is the object of the preposition. Here are some common prepositions:

about	as	at	after
by	for	from	in
of	on	to	with

Verbals and Verbal Phrases

Verbals are forms of verbs that act as other parts of speech. They can be used as nouns, adjectives, or adverbs. Though they are use verb forms, they are not to be used as the verb in the sentence. A word group that is based on a verbal is considered a *verbal phrase*. There are three major types of verbals: *participles, gerunds,* and *infinitives.*

Participles are verbals that act as adjectives. The present participle ends in *–ing*, and the past participle ends in *–d*, *-ed*, *-n*, or-*t*.

Verb	Present Participle	Past Participle
walk	walking	walked
share	sharing	shared

Participial phrases are made up of the participle and modifiers, complements, or objects.

Crying for most of an hour, the baby didn't seem to want to nap.

Having already taken this course, the student was bored during class.

Crying for most of an hour and *Having already taken this course* are the participial phrases.

Gerunds are verbals that are used as nouns and end in *–ing*. A gerund can be the subject or object of the sentence like a noun. Note that a present participle can also end in *–ing*, so it is important to distinguish between the two. The gerund is used as a noun, while the participle is used as an adjective.

Swimming is my favorite sport.

I wish I were sleeping.

A *gerund phrase* includes the gerund and any modifiers or complements, direct objects, indirect objects, or pronouns.

Cleaning the house is my least favorite weekend activity.

Cleaning the house is the gerund phrase acting as the subject of the sentence.

The most important goal this year is raising money for charity.

Raising money for charity is the gerund phrase acting as the direct object.

The police accused the woman of stealing the car.

The *gerund* phrase *stealing the car* is the object of the preposition in this sentence.

An *infinitive* is a verbal made up of the word to and a verb. Infinitives can be used as nouns, adjectives, or adverbs.

Examples: To eat, to jump, to swim, to lie, to call, to work

An *infinitive phrase* is made up of the infinitive plus any complements or modifiers. The infinitive phrase *to wait* is used as the subject in this sentence:

To wait was not what I had in mind.

The infinitive phrase *to sing* is used as the subject complement in this sentence:

Her dream is to sing.

The infinitive phrase *to grow* is used as an adverb in this sentence:

Children must eat to grow.

Appositive Phrases

An *appositive* is a noun or noun phrase that renames a noun that comes immediately before it in the sentence. An appositive can be a single word or several words. These phrases can be *essential* or *nonessential*. An essential appositive phrase is necessary to the meaning of the sentence and a nonessential appositive phrase is not. It is important to be able to distinguish these for purposes of comma use.

Essential: My sister Christina works at a school.

Naming which sister is essential to the meaning of the sentence, so no commas are needed.

Nonessential: My sister, who is a teacher, is coming over for dinner tonight.

Who is a teacher is not essential to the meaning of the sentence, so commas are required.

Absolute Phrases

An *absolute phrase* modifies a noun without using a conjunction. It is not the subject of the sentence and is not a complete thought on its own. Absolute phrases are set off from the independent clause with a comma.

Arms outstretched, she yelled at the sky.

All things considered, this has been a great day.

The Four Types of Sentence Structures

A *simple sentence* has one independent clause.

I am going to win.

A *compound sentence* has two independent clauses. A conjunction—*for, and, nor, but, or, yet, so*—links them together. Note that each of the independent clauses has a subject and a verb.

I am going to win, but the odds are against me.

A *complex sentence* has one independent clause and one or more dependent clauses.

I am going to win, even though I don't deserve it.

Even though I don't deserve it is a dependent clause. It does not stand on its own. Some conjunctions that link an independent and a dependent clause are *although, because, before, after, that, when, which*, and *while*.

A *compound-complex sentence* has at least three clauses, two of which are independent and at least one that is a dependent clause.

While trying to dance, I tripped over my partner's feet, but I regained my balance quickly.

The dependent clause is *While trying to dance*.

Sentence Fragments

A *sentence fragment* is an incomplete sentence. An independent clause is made up of a subject and a predicate, and both are needed to make a complete sentence.

Sentence fragments often begin with relative pronouns (when, which), subordinating conjunctions (because, although) or gerunds (trying, being, seeing). They might be missing the subject or the predicate.

The most common type of fragment is the isolated dependent clause, which can be corrected by joining it to the independent clause that appears before or after the fragment:

Fragment: While the cookies baked.

Correction: While the cookies baked, we played cards. (We played cards while the cookies baked.)

Run-on Sentences

A *run-on sentence* is created when two independent clauses (complete thoughts) are joined without correct punctuation or a conjunction. Run-on sentences can be corrected in the following ways:

- Join the independent clauses with a comma and coordinating conjunction.

  Run-on: We forgot to return the library books we had to pay a fine.

  Correction: We forgot to return the library books, so we had to pay a fine.

- Join the independent clauses with a semicolon, dash, or colon when the clauses are closely related in meaning.

  Run-on: I had a salad for lunch every day this week I feel healthier already.

  Correction: I had a salad for lunch every day this week; I feel healthier already.

- Join the independent clauses with a *semicolon and a conjunctive adverb.*

  Run-on: We arrived at the animal shelter on time however the dog had already been adopted.

  Correction: We arrived at the animal shelter on time; however, the dog had already been adopted.

- Separate the independent clauses into two sentences *with a period.*

  Run-on: He tapes his favorite television show he never misses an episode.

  Correction: He tapes his favorite television show. He never misses an episode.

- *Rearrange the wording* of the sentence to create an independent clause and a dependent clause.

  Run-on: My wedding date is coming up I am getting more excited to walk down the aisle.

  Correction: As my wedding date approaches, I am getting more excited to walk down the aisle.

Dangling and Misplaced Modifiers

A *modifier* is a phrase that describes, alters, limits, or gives more information about a word in the sentence. The two most common issues are dangling and misplaced modifiers.

A *dangling modifier* is created when the phrase modifies a word that is not clearly stated in the sentence.

Dangling modifier: Having finished dinner, the dishes were cleared from the table.

Correction: Having finished dinner, Amy cleared the dishes from the table.

In the first sentence, *having finished dinner* appears to modify *the dishes*, which obviously can't finish dinner. The second sentence adds the subject *Amy*, to make it clear who has finished dinner.

Dangling modifier: Hoping to improve test scores, all new books were ordered for the school.

Correction: Hoping to improve test scores, administrators ordered all new books for the school.

Without the subject *administrators*, it appears the books are hoping to improve test scores, which doesn't make sense.

Misplaced modifiers are placed incorrectly in the sentence, which can cause confusion. Compare these examples:

Misplaced modifier: Rory purchased a new flat screen television and placed it on the wall above the fireplace, with all the bells and whistles.

Revised: Rory purchased a new flat screen television, with all the bells and whistles, and placed it on the wall above the fireplace.

The bells and whistles should modify the television, not the fireplace.

Misplaced modifier: The delivery driver arrived late with the pizza, who was usually on time.

Revised: The delivery driver, who usually was on time, arrived late with the pizza.

This suggests that the delivery driver was usually on time, instead of the pizza.

Misplaced modifier: We saw a family of ducks on the way to church.

Revised: On the way to church, we saw a family of ducks.

The misplaced modifier, here, suggests the *ducks* were on their way to church, instead of the pronoun *we*.

Split Infinitives

An infinitive is made up of the word *to* and a verb, such as: to run, to jump, to ask. A *split infinitive* is created when a word comes between *to* and the verb.

Split infinitive: To quickly run

Correction: To run quickly

Split infinitive: To quietly ask

Correction: To ask quietly

Double Negatives

A *double negative* is a negative statement that includes two negative elements. This is incorrect in Standard English.

Incorrect: She hasn't never come to my house to visit.

Correct: She has never come to my house to visit.

The intended meaning is that she has never come to the house, so the double negative is incorrect. However, it is possible to use two negatives to create a positive statement.

Correct: She was not unhappy with her performance on the quiz.

In this case, the double negative*, was not unhappy*, is intended to show a positive, so it is correct. This means that she was somewhat happy with her performance.

Faulty Parallelism

It is necessary to use parallel construction in sentences that have multiple similar ideas. Using parallel structure provides clarity in writing. *Faulty parallelism* is created when multiple ideas are joined using different sentence structures. Compare these examples:

Incorrect: We start each practice with stretches, a run, and fielding grounders.
Correct: We start each practice with stretching, running, and fielding grounders.

Incorrect: I watched some television, reading my book, and fell asleep.
Correct: I watched some television, read my book, and fell asleep.

Incorrect: *Some of the readiness skills for Kindergarten are to cut with scissors, to tie shoes, and dressing independently.*
Correct: *Some of the readiness skills for Kindergarten are being able to cut with scissors, to tie shoes, and to dress independently.*

Subordination

If multiple pieces of information in a sentence are not equal, they can be joined by creating an independent clause and a dependent clause. The less important information becomes the *subordinate clause*:

Draft: The hotel was acceptable. We wouldn't stay at the hotel again.

Revised: Though the hotel was acceptable, we wouldn't stay there again.

The more important information (*we wouldn't stay there again*) becomes the main clause, and the less important information (*the hotel was acceptable*) becomes the subordinate clause.

Context Clues

Context clues help readers understand unfamiliar words, and thankfully, there are many types.

Synonyms are words or phrases that have nearly, if not exactly, the same meaning as other words or phrases

> *Large* boxes are needed to pack *big* items.

Antonyms are words or phrases that have opposite definitions. Antonyms, like synonyms, can serve as context clues, although more cryptically.

> *Large* boxes are not needed to pack *small* items.

Definitions are sometimes included within a sentence to define uncommon words.

> They practiced the *rumba*, a *type of dance*, for hours on end.

Explanations provide context through elaboration.

> Large boxes holding items weighing over 60 pounds were stacked in the corner.

Here's an example of *contrast*:

> These *minute* creatures were much different than the *huge* mammals that the zoologist was accustomed to dealing with.

Beware of Simplicity

Sometimes the answer may seem very simple. In this case, it's prudent to look more carefully at the question and the possible answer choices. Very brief answers aren't always correct, and the opposite may also be true. The goal is to read all the answer choices carefully, trying to rule out those that don't make sense.

Final Notes

It's best to read every answer choice before making a decision. While some answers may seem plausible, there may be others that are better choices. First instinct is usually right, but reading every answer is recommended. Caution should be taken in choosing an answer that "sounds right." Grammar rules can be tricky, and what sounds right may not be correct. It's best to rely on knowledge of grammar to choose the best answer. Ruling out incorrect responses can help narrow the choices down. Choosing between two choices (after reading them carefully) and selecting the answer that best matches the rules of Standard English is less overwhelming.

WritePlacer

Brainstorming

One of the most important steps in writing an essay is prewriting. Before drafting an essay, it's helpful to think about the topic for a moment or two, in order to gain a more solid understanding of what the task is. Then, spending about five minutes jotting down the immediate ideas that could work for the essay is recommended. It is a way to get some words on the page and offer a reference for ideas when drafting. Scratch paper is provided for writers to use any prewriting techniques such as webbing, free writing, or listing. The goal is to get ideas out of the mind and onto the page.

Considering Opposing Viewpoints

In the planning stage, it's important to consider all aspects of the topic, including different viewpoints on the subject. There are more than two ways to look at a topic, and a strong argument considers those opposing viewpoints. Considering opposing viewpoints can help writers present a fair, balanced, and informed essay that shows consideration for all readers. This approach can also strengthen an argument by recognizing and potentially refuting the opposing viewpoint(s).

Drawing from personal experience may help to support ideas. For example, if the goal for writing is a personal narrative, then the story should be from the writer's own life. Many writers find it helpful to draw from personal experience, even in an essay that is not strictly narrative. Personal anecdotes or short stories can help to illustrate a point in other types of essays as well.

Moving from Brainstorming to Planning

Once the ideas are on the page, it's time to turn them into a solid plan for the essay. The best ideas from the brainstorming results can then be developed into a more formal outline. An outline typically has one main point (the thesis) and at least three sub-points that support the main point. Here's an example:

Main Idea

- Point #1
- Point #2
- Point #3

Of course, there will be details under each point, but this approach is the best for dealing with timed writing.

Staying on Track

Basing the essay on the outline aids in both organization and coherence. The goal is to ensure that there is enough time to develop each sub-point in the essay, roughly spending an equal amount of time on each idea. Keeping an eye on the time will help. If there are fifteen minutes left to draft the essay, then it makes sense to spend about 5 minutes on each of the ideas. Staying on task is critical to success, and timing out the parts of the essay can help writers avoid feeling overwhelmed.

Parts of the Essay

The *introduction* has to do a few important things:

- Establish the *topic* of the essay in original wording (i.e., not just repeating the prompt)
- Clarify the significance/importance of the topic or purpose for writing (not too many details, a brief overview)
- Offer a *thesis statement* that identifies the writer's own viewpoint on the topic (typically one-two brief sentences as a clear, concise explanation of the main point on the topic)

Body paragraphs reflect the ideas developed in the outline. Three-four points is probably sufficient for a short essay, and they should include the following:

- A *topic sentence* that identifies the sub-point (e.g., a reason why, a way how, a cause or effect)
- A detailed *explanation* of the point, explaining why the writer thinks this point is valid
- Illustrative examples, such as personal examples or real-world examples, that support and validate the point (i.e., "prove" the point)
- A *concluding sentence* that connects the examples, reasoning, and analysis to the point being made

The *conclusion*, or final paragraph, should be brief and should reiterate the focus, clarifying why the discussion is significant or important. It is important to avoid adding specific details or new ideas to this paragraph. The purpose of the conclusion is to sum up what has been said to bring the discussion to a close.

Don't Panic!

Writing an essay can be overwhelming, and performance panic is a natural response. The outline serves as a basis for the writing and help writers keep focused. Getting stuck can also happen, and it's helpful to remember that brainstorming can be done at any time during the writing process. Following the steps of the writing process is the best defense against writer's block.

Timed essays can be particularly stressful, but assessors are trained to recognize the necessary planning and thinking for these timed efforts. Using the plan above and sticking to it helps with time management. Timing each part of the process helps writers stay on track. Sometimes writers try to cover too much in their essays. If time seems to be running out, this is an opportunity to determine whether all of the ideas in the outline are necessary. Three body paragraphs are sufficient, and more than that is probably too much to cover in a short essay.

More isn't always *better* in writing. A strong essay will be clear and concise. It will avoid unnecessary or repetitive details. It is better to have a concise, five-paragraph essay that makes a clear point, than a ten-paragraph essay that doesn't. The goal is to write one-two pages of quality writing. Paragraphs should also reflect balance; if the introduction goes to the bottom of the first page, the writing may be going off-track or be repetitive. It's best to fall into the one-two page range, but a complete, well-developed essay is the ultimate goal.

The Final Steps

Leaving a few minutes at the end to revise and proofread offers an opportunity for writers to polish things up. Putting one's self in the reader's shoes and focusing on what the essay actually says helps writers identify problems—it's a movement from the mindset of writer to the mindset of editor. The goal is to have a clean, clear copy of the essay. The following areas should be considered when proofreading:

- Sentence fragments
- Awkward sentence structure
- Run-on sentences
- Incorrect word choice
- Grammatical agreement errors
- Spelling errors
- Punctuation errors
- Capitalization errors

The Short Overview

The essay may seem challenging, but following these steps can help writers focus:

- Take one-two minutes to think about the topic.
- Generate some ideas through brainstorming (three-four minutes).
- Organize ideas into a brief outline, selecting just three-four main points to cover in the essay (eventually the body paragraphs).
- Develop essay in parts:
- Introduction paragraph, with intro to topic and main points
- Viewpoint on the subject at the end of the introduction
- Body paragraphs, based on outline
- Each paragraph: makes a main point, explains the viewpoint, uses examples to support the point
- Brief conclusion highlighting the main points and closing
- Read over the essay (last five minutes).
- Look for any obvious errors, making sure that the writing makes sense.

Accuplacer English Practice Test #1

Reading Comprehension

Directions for questions 1–10

Read the statement or passage and then choose the best answer to the question. Answer the question based on what is stated or implied in the statement or passage.

1. While scientists aren't entirely certain why tornadoes form, they have some clues into the process. Tornadoes are dangerous funnel clouds that occur during a large thunderstorm. When warm, humid air near the ground meets cold, dry air from above, a column of the warm air can be drawn up into the clouds. Winds at different altitudes blowing at different speeds make the column of air rotate. As the spinning column of air picks up speed, a funnel cloud is formed. This funnel cloud moves rapidly and haphazardly. Rain and hail inside the cloud cause it to touch down, creating a tornado. Tornadoes move in a rapid and unpredictable pattern, making them extremely destructive and dangerous. Scientists continue to study tornadoes to improve radar detection and warning times.

The main purpose of this passage is to:

a. Show why tornadoes are dangerous
b. Explain how a tornado forms
c. Compare thunderstorms to tornadoes
d. Explain what to do in the event of a tornado

2. There are two major kinds of cameras on the market right now for amateur photographers. Camera enthusiasts can either purchase a digital single-lens reflex camera (DSLR) camera or a compact system camera (CSC). The main difference between a DSLR and a CSC is that the DSLR has a full-sized sensor, which means it fits in a much larger body. The CSC uses a mirrorless system, which makes for a lighter, smaller camera. While both take quality pictures, the DSLR generally has better picture quality due to the larger sensor. CSCs still take very good quality pictures and are more convenient to carry than a DSLR. This makes the CSC an ideal choice for the amateur photographer looking to step up from a point-and-shoot camera.

The main difference between the DSLR and CSC is:

a. The picture quality is better in the DSLR.
b. The CSC is less expensive than the DSLR.
c. The DSLR is a better choice for amateur photographers.
d. The DSLR's larger sensor makes it a bigger camera than the CSC.

3. When selecting a career path, it's important to explore the various options available. Many students entering college may shy away from a major because they don't know much about it. For example, many students won't opt for a career as an actuary, because they aren't exactly sure what it entails. They would be missing out on a career that is very lucrative and in high demand. Actuaries work in the insurance field and assess risks and premiums. The average salary of an actuary is $100,000 per year. Another career option students may avoid, due to lack of knowledge of the field, is a hospitalist. This is a physician that specializes in the care of patients in a hospital, as opposed to those seen in private

practices. The average salary of a hospitalist is upwards of $200,000. It pays to do some digging and find out more about these lesser-known career fields.

An actuary is:

a. A doctor who works in a hospital
b. The same as a hospitalist
c. An insurance agent who works in a hospital
d. A person who assesses insurance risks and premiums

4. Many people are unsure of exactly how the digestive system works. Digestion begins in the mouth where teeth grind up food and saliva breaks it down, making it easier for the body to absorb. Next, the food moves to the esophagus, and it is pushed into the stomach. The stomach is where food is stored and broken down further by acids and digestive enzymes, preparing it for passage into the intestines. The small intestine is where the nutrients are taken from food and passed into the blood stream. Other essential organs like the liver, gall bladder, and pancreas aid the stomach in breaking down food and absorbing nutrients. Finally, food waste is passed into the large intestine where it is eliminated by the body.

The purpose of this passage is to:

a. Explain how the liver works.
b. Show why it is important to eat healthy foods
c. Explain how the digestive system works
d. Show how nutrients are absorbed by the small intestine

5. Hard water occurs when rainwater mixes with minerals from rock and soil. Hard water has a high mineral count, including calcium and magnesium. The mineral deposits from hard water can stain hard surfaces in bathrooms and kitchens as well as clog pipes. Hard water can stain dishes, ruin clothes, and reduce the life of any appliances it touches, such as hot water heaters, washing machines, and humidifiers.

One solution is to install a water softener to reduce the mineral content of water, but this can be costly. Running vinegar through pipes and appliances and using vinegar to clean hard surfaces can also help with mineral deposits.

From this passage, it can be concluded that:

a. Hard water can cause a lot of problems for homeowners.
b. Calcium is good for pipes and hard surfaces.
c. Water softeners are easy to install.
d. Vinegar is the only solution to hard water problems.

6. Osteoporosis is a medical condition that occurs when the body loses bone or makes too little bone. This can lead to brittle, fragile bones that easily break. Bones are already porous, and when osteoporosis sets in, the spaces in bones become much larger, causing them to weaken. Both men and women can contract osteoporosis, though it is most common in women over age 50. Loss of bone can be silent and progressive, so it is important to be proactive in prevention of the disease.

The main purpose of this passage is to:
- a. Discuss some of the ways people contract osteoporosis
- b. Describe different treatment options for those with osteoporosis
- c. Explain how to prevent osteoporosis
- d. Define osteoporosis

7. Vacationers looking for a perfect experience should opt out of Disney parks and try a trip on Disney Cruise Lines. While a park offers rides, characters, and show experiences, it also includes long lines, often very hot weather, and enormous crowds. A Disney Cruise, on the other hand, is a relaxing, luxurious vacation that includes many of the same experiences as the parks, minus the crowds and lines. The cruise has top-notch food, maid service, water slides, multiple pools, Broadway-quality shows, and daily character experiences for kids. There are also many activities, such as bingo, trivia contests, and dance parties that can entertain guests of all ages. The cruise even stops at Disney's private island for a beach barbecue with characters, waterslides, and water sports. Those looking for the Disney experience without the hassle should book a Disney cruise.

The main purpose of this passage is to:
- a. Explain how to book a Disney cruise
- b. Show what Disney parks have to offer
- c. Show why Disney parks are expensive
- d. Compare Disney parks to the Disney cruise

8. Coaches of kids' sports teams are increasingly concerned about the behavior of parents at games. Parents are screaming and cursing at coaches, officials, players, and other parents. Physical fights have even broken out at games. Parents need to be reminded that coaches are volunteers, giving up their time and energy to help kids develop in their chosen sport. The goal of kids' sports teams is to learn and develop skills, but it's also to have fun. When parents are out of control at games and practices, it takes the fun out of the sport.

From this passage, it can be concluded that:
- a. Coaches are modeling good behavior for kids.
- b. Organized sports are not good for kids.
- c. Parents' behavior at their kids' games needs to change.
- d. Parents and coaches need to work together.

9. As summer approaches, drowning incidents will increase. Drowning happens very quickly and silently. Most people assume that drowning is easy to spot, but a person who is drowning doesn't make noise or wave his arms. Instead, he will have his head back and his mouth open, with just his face out of the water. A person who is truly in danger of drowning is not able to wave his arms in the air or move much at all. Recognizing these signs of drowning can prevent tragedy.

The main purpose of this passage is to:

a. Explain the dangers of swimming
b. Show how to identify the signs of drowning
c. Explain how to be a lifeguard
d. Compare the signs of drowning

10. Technology has been invading cars for the last several years, but there are some new high tech trends that are pretty amazing. It is now standard in many car models to have a rear-view camera, hands-free phone and text, and a touch screen digital display. Music can be streamed from a paired cell phone, and some displays can even be programmed with a personal photo. Sensors beep to indicate there is something in the driver's path when reversing and changing lanes. Rain-sensing windshield wipers and lights are automatic, leaving the driver with little to do but watch the road and enjoy the ride. The next wave of technology will include cars that automatically parallel park, and a self-driving car is on the horizon. These technological advances make it a good time to be a driver.

It can be concluded from this paragraph that:

a. Technology will continue to influence how cars are made.
b. Windshield wipers and lights are always automatic.
c. It is standard to have a rear-view camera in all cars.
d. Technology has reached its peak in cars.

Directions for questions 11–20

For the questions that follow, two underlined sentences are followed by a question or statement. Read the sentences, then choose the best answer to the question or the best completion of the statement.

11. The NBA draft process is based on a lottery system among the teams who did not make the playoffs in the previous season to determine draft order. Only the top three draft picks are determined by the lottery.

What does the second sentence do?

a. It contradicts the first.
b. It supports the first.
c. It restates information from the first.
d. It offers a solution.

12. While many people use multiple social media sites, Facebook remains the most popular with more than one billion users. Instagram is rising in popularity and, with 100 million users, is now the most-used social media site.

What does the second sentence do?

a. It expands on the first.
b. It contradicts the first.
c. It supports the first.
d. It proposes a solution.

13. There are eight different phases of the moon, from new moon to new moon. One of the eight different moon phases is first quarter, commonly called a half moon.

What does the second sentence do?

a. It provides an example.
b. It contradicts the first.
c. It states an effect.
d. It offers a solution.

14. The terror attacks of September 11, 2001 have had many lasting effects on the United States. The Department of Homeland Security was created in late September 2001 in response to the terror attacks and became an official cabinet-level department in November of 2002.

What does the second sentence do?

a. It contradicts the first.
b. It restates the information from the first.
c. It states an effect.
d. It makes a contrast.

15. Annuals are plants that complete the life cycle in a single growing season. Perennials are plants that complete the life cycle in many growing seasons, dying in the winter and coming back each spring.

What does the second sentence do?

a. It makes a contrast.
b. It disputes the first sentence.
c. It provides an example.
d. It states an effect.

16. Personal computers can be subject to viruses and malware, which can lead to slow performance, loss of files, and overheating. Antivirus software is often sold along with a new PC to protect against viruses and malware.

What does the second sentence do?

a. It makes a contrast.
b. It provides an example.
c. It restates the information from the first.
d. It offers a solution.

17. Many companies tout their chicken as cage-free because the chickens are not confined to small wire cages. However, cage-free chickens are often crammed into buildings with thousands of other birds and never go outside in their short lifetime.

What does the second sentence do?

a. It offers a solution.
b. It provides an example.
c. It disputes the first sentence.
d. It states an effect.

18. Common core standards do not include the instruction of cursive handwriting. The next generation of students will not be able to read or write cursive handwriting.

What does the second sentence do?

a. It offers a solution.
b. It states an effect.
c. It contradicts the first sentence.
d. It restates the first sentence.

19. Air travel has changed significantly in the last ten years. Airlines are now offering pay-as-you-go perks, including no baggage fees, seat selection, and food and drinks on the flight to keep costs low.

What does the second sentence do?

a. It states effects.
b. It provides examples.
c. It disputes the first sentence.
d. It offers solutions.

20. Many people are unaware that fragrances and other chemicals in their favorite products are causing skin reactions and allergies. Surprisingly, many popular products contain ingredients that can cause skin allergies.

What does the second sentence do?

a. It restates the first sentence.
b. It provides examples.
c. It contradicts the first sentence.
d. It provides solutions.

Sentence Skills

Sentence Correction

Directions for questions 1–10

Select the best version of the underlined part of the sentence. The first choice is the same as the original sentence. If you think the original sentence is best, choose the first answer.

1. An important issues stemming from this meeting is that we won't have enough time to meet all of the objectives.

   a. An important issues stemming from this meeting
   b. Important issue stemming from this meeting
   c. An important issue stemming from this meeting
   d. Important issues stemming from this meeting

2. The rising popularity of the clean eating movement can be attributed to the fact that experts say added sugars and chemicals in our food are to blame for the obesity epidemic.

   a. to the fact that experts say added sugars and chemicals in our food are to blame for the obesity epidemic.
   b. in the facts that experts say added sugars and chemicals in our food are to blame for the obesity epidemic.
   c. to the fact that experts saying added sugars and chemicals in our food are to blame for the obesity epidemic.
   d. with the facts that experts say added sugars and chemicals in our food are to blame for the obesity epidemic.

3. She's looking for a suitcase that can fit all of her clothes, shoes, accessory, and makeup.

   a. clothes, shoes, accessory, and makeup.
   b. clothes, shoes, accessories, and makeup.
   c. clothes, shoes, accessories, and makeups.
   d. clothes, shoe, accessory, and makeup.

4. Shawn started taking guitar lessons while he wanted to become a better musician.

   a. while he wanted to become a better musician.
   b. because he wants to become a better musician.
   c. even though he wanted to become a better musician.
   d. because he wanted to become a better musician.

5. Considering the recent rains we have had, it's a wonder the plants haven't drowned.

   a. Considering the recent rains we have had, it's a wonder
   b. Consider the recent rains we have had, it's a wonder
   c. Considering for how much recent rain we have had, its a wonder
   d. Considering, the recent rains we have had, its a wonder

6. Since none of the furniture were delivered on time, we have to move in at a later date.

   a. Since none of the furniture were delivered on time,
   b. Since none of the furniture was delivered on time,
   c. Since all of the furniture were delivered on time,
   d. Since all of the furniture was delivered on time

7. It is necessary for instructors to offer tutoring to any students who need extra help in the class.

   a. to any students who need extra help in the class.
   b. for any students that need extra help in the class.
   c. with any students who need extra help in the class.
   d. for any students needing any extra help in their class.

8. The fact the train set only includes four cars and one small track was a big disappointment to my son.

a. the train set only includes four cars and one small track was a big disappointment
b. that the trains set only include four cars and one small track was a big disappointment
c. that the train set only includes four cars and one small track was a big disappointment
d. that the train set only includes four cars and one small track were a big disappointment

9. Because many people feel there are too many distractions to get any work done, I actually enjoy working from home.

a. Because many people
b. While many people
c. Maybe many people
d. With most people

10. There were many questions about what causes the case to have gone cold, but the detective wasn't willing to discuss it with reporters.

a. about what causes the case to have gone cold
b. about why the case is cold
c. about what causes the case to go cold
d. about why the case went cold

Construction Shift

Directions for questions 11–20

Rewrite the sentence in your head following the directions given below. Keep in mind that your new sentence should be well written and should have essentially the same meaning as the original sentence.

11. Although she was nervous speaking in front of a crowd, the author read her narrative with poise and confidence.

Rewrite, beginning with

The author had poise and confidence while reading

The next words will be

a. because she was nervous speaking in front of a crowd.
b. but she was nervous speaking in front of a crowd.
c. even though she was nervous speaking in front of a crowd.
d. before she was nervous speaking in front of a crowd.

12. There was a storm surge and loss of electricity during the hurricane.

Rewrite, beginning with

While the hurricane occurred,

The next words will be

a. there was a storm surge after the electricity went out.
b. the storm surge caused the electricity to go out.
c. the electricity surged into the storm.
d. the electricity went out and there was a storm surge.

13. When one elephant in a herd is sick, the rest of the herd will help it walk and bring it food.

Rewrite, beginning with

An elephant herd will

The next words will be

a. be too sick and tired to walk
b. help and support
c. gather food when they're sick
d. be unable to walk without food

14. They went out to eat after the soccer game.

Rewrite, beginning with

They finished the soccer game

The next words will be

a. then went out to eat.
b. after they went out to eat.
c. so they could go out to eat.
d. because they went out to eat.

15. Armani got lost when she walked around Paris.

Rewrite, beginning with

Walking through Paris,

The next words will be

a. you can get lost.
b. Armani found herself lost.
c. she should have gotten lost.
d. is about getting lost.

16. After his cat died, Phoenix buried the cat with her favorite toys in his backyard.

Rewrite, beginning with

Phoenix buried his cat

The next words will be

a. in his backyard before she died.
b. after she died in the backyard.
c. with her favorite toys after she died.
d. after he buried her toys in the backyard.

17. While I was in the helicopter I saw the sunset, and tears streamed down my eyes.

Rewrite, beginning with

Tears streamed down my eyes

The next words will be:

a. while I watched the helicopter fly into the sunset.
b. because the sunset flew up into the sky.
c. because the helicopter was facing the sunset.
d. when I saw the sunset from the helicopter.

18. I won't go to the party unless some of my friends go.

Rewrite, beginning with

I will go the party

The next words will be

a. if I want to.
b. if my friends go.
c. since a couple of my friends are going.
d. unless people I know go.

19. He had a broken leg before the car accident, so it took him a long time to recover.

Rewrite, beginning with

He took a long time to recover from the car accident

The next words will be

a. from his two broken legs.
b. after he broke his leg.
c. because he already had a broken leg.
d. since he broke his leg again afterward.

20. We had a party the day after Halloween to celebrate my birthday.

Rewrite, beginning with

It was my birthday.

The next words will be

a. , so we celebrated with a party the day after Halloween.
b. the day of Halloween so we celebrated with a party.
c. , and we celebrated with a Halloween party the day after.
d. a few days before Halloween, so we threw a party.

Practice Prompt

Prepare an essay of about 300–600 words on the topic below.

> Some people feel that sharing their lives on social media sites such as Facebook, Instagram, and Snapchat is fine. They share every aspect of their lives, including pictures of themselves and their families, what they ate for lunch, who they are dating, and when they are going on vacation. They even say that if it's not on social media, it didn't happen. Other people believe that sharing so much personal information is an invasion of privacy and could prove dangerous. They think sharing personal pictures and details invites predators, cyberbullying, and identity theft.

Write an essay to someone who is considering whether to participate in social media. Take a side on the issue and argue whether or not he/she should join a social media network. Use specific examples to support your argument.

Answer Explanations #1

Reading Comprehension

1. B: The main point of this passage is to show how a tornado forms. Choice *A* is off base because while the passage does mention that tornadoes are dangerous, it is not the main focus of the passage. While thunderstorms are mentioned, they are not compared to tornadoes, so Choice *C* is incorrect. Choice *D* is incorrect because the passage does not discuss what to do in the event of a tornado.

2. D: The passage directly states that the larger sensor is the main difference between the two cameras. Choices *A* and *B* may be true, but these answers do not identify the major difference between the two cameras. Choice *C* states the opposite of what the paragraph suggests is the best option for amateur photographers, so it is incorrect.

3. D: An actuary assesses risks and sets insurance premiums. While an actuary does work in insurance, the passage does not suggest that actuaries have any affiliation with hospitalists or working in a hospital, so all other choices are incorrect.

4. C: The purpose of this passage is to explain how the digestive system works. Choice *A* focuses only on the liver, which is a small part of the process and not the focus of the paragraph. Choice *B* is off-track because the passage does not mention healthy foods. Choice *D* only focuses on one part of the digestive system.

5. A: The passage focuses mainly on the problems of hard water. Choice *B* is incorrect because calcium is not good for pipes and hard surfaces. The passage does not say anything about whether water softeners are easy to install, so *C* is incorrect. *D* is also incorrect because the passage does offer other solutions besides vinegar.

6. D: The main point of this passage is to define osteoporosis. Choice *A* is incorrect because the passage does not list ways that people contract osteoporosis. Choice *B* is incorrect because the passage does not mention any treatment options. While the passage does briefly mention prevention, it does not explain how, so Choice *C* is incorrect.

7. D: The passage compares Disney cruises with Disney parks. It does not discuss how to book a cruise, so Choice *A* is incorrect. Choice *B* is incorrect because though the passage does mention some of the park attractions, it is not the main point. The passage does not mention the cost of either option, so Choice *C* is incorrect.

8. C: The main point of this paragraph is that parents need to change their poor behavior at their kids' sporting events. Choice *A* is incorrect because the coaches' behavior is not mentioned in the paragraph. *B* suggests that sports are bad for kids, when the paragraph is about parents' behavior, so it is incorrect. While Choice *D* may be true, it offers a specific solution to the problem, which the paragraph does not discuss.

9. B: The point of this passage is to show what drowning looks like. Choice *A* is incorrect because while drowning is a danger of swimming, the passage doesn't include any other dangers. The passage is not intended for lifeguards specifically, but for a general audience, so Choice *C* is incorrect. There are a few signs of drowning, but the passage does not compare them; thus, Choice *D* is incorrect.

10. A: The passage discusses recent technological advances in cars and suggests that this trend will continue in the future with self-driving cars. Choice *B* and *C* are not true, so these are both incorrect. Choice *D* is also incorrect because the passage suggests continuing growth in technology, not a peak.

11. B: The information in the second sentence further explains the draft process and thus supports the first sentence. It does not contradict the first sentence, so *A* is incorrect. Choice *C* and *D* are incorrect because the second sentence does not restate or offer a solution to the first.

12. B: The first sentence identifies Facebook as the most popular social media site with 1 billion users. The second sentence states that Instagram only has 100 million users, but is the most used. This contradicts the original sentence, so all other answers are incorrect.

13. A: The first sentence states that there are eight phases to the moon cycle. The second sentence discusses first quarter, which is one of the phases of the moon. Therefore, the second sentence provides an example of the first sentence.

14. C: The first sentence discusses the effects of the terror attacks of September 11, 2001. The second sentence states that the Department of Homeland Security was created in response to the terror attacks, so it states an effect of the first sentence.

15. A: The first sentence describes the life cycle of annuals. The second sentence describes the life cycle of perennials, making a contrast between the way annuals grow and the way perennials grow.

16. D: The first sentence describes how viruses can affect a PC. The second sentence offers a solution to the problem of viruses and malware on a PC.

17. C: The first sentence describes cage-free chickens as not being confined to a cage, suggesting they are treated humanely. The second sentence disputes the first sentence, showing that cage-free chickens are inhumanely confined to a larger area with many other chickens, never seeing the outdoors.

18. B: The first sentence states that schools are no longer teaching cursive handwriting. The second sentence shows that as an effect of the first sentence, students will no longer be able to read or write cursive handwriting.

19. B: The first sentence states that air travel has changed in the last decade. The second sentence provides examples of the changes that have occurred.

20. A: The first sentence discusses how fragrances and other chemicals in products can cause skin reactions. The second sentence states that many products contain ingredients that cause skin allergies, restating the same information from the first sentence.

Sentence Skills

Sentence Correction

1. C: In this answer, the article and subject agree, and the subject and predicate agree. Choice *C* is incorrect because the article (*an*) and the noun (*issues*) do not agree in number. Choice *B* is incorrect because an article is needed before *important issue*. Choice *D* is incorrect because the plural subject *issues* does not agree with the singular verb *is*.

2. A: Choices *B* and *D* both use the expression *attributed to the fact* incorrectly. It can only be attributed *to* the fact, not *with* or *in* the fact. Choice *C* incorrectly uses a gerund, *saying*, when it should use the present tense of the verb *say*.

3. B: Choice *B* is correct because it uses correct parallel structure of plural nouns. *A* is incorrect because the word *accessory* is in singular form. Choice *C* is incorrect because it pluralizes *makeup*, which is already in plural form. Choice *D* is incorrect because it again uses the singular *accessory*, and it uses the singular *shoe*.

4: In a cause/effect relationship, it is correct to use word *because* in the clausal part of the sentence. This can eliminate both Choices *A and* C which don't clearly show the cause/effect relationship. Choice *B* is incorrect because it uses the present tense, when the first part of the sentence is in the past tense. It makes grammatical sense for both parts of the sentence to be in present tense.

5. A: In Choice *B*, the present tense form of the verb *consider* creates an independent clause joined to another independent clause with only a comma, which is a comma splice and grammatically incorrect. Both *C* and *D* use the possessive form of *its*, when it should be the contraction *it's* for *it is*. Choice *D* also includes incorrect comma placement.

6. B: Choice *A* uses the plural form of the verb, when the subject is the pronoun *none*, which needs a singular verb. Choice *C* also uses the wrong verb form and uses the word *all* in place of *none*, which doesn't make sense in the context of the sentence. Choice *D* uses *all* again, and is missing the comma, which is necessary to set the dependent clause off from the independent clause.

7. A: Answer Choice *A* uses the best, most concise word choice. Choice *B* uses the pronoun *that* to refer to people instead of *who*. *C* incorrectly uses the preposition *with*. Choice *D* uses the preposition *for* and the additional word *any*, making the sentence wordy and less clear.

8. C: Choice *A* is missing the word *that*, which is necessary for the sentence to make sense. Choice *B* pluralizes *trains* and uses the singular form of the word *include*, so it does not agree with the word *set*. Choice *D* changes the verb to *were*, which is in plural form and does not agree with the singular subject.

9. B: Choice *B* uses the best choice of words to create a subordinate and independent clause. In Choice *A*, *because* makes it seem like this is the reason I enjoy working from home, which is incorrect. In *C*, the word *maybe* creates two independent clauses, which are not joined properly with a comma. Choice *D* uses *with*, which does not make grammatical sense.

10. D: Choices *A* and *C* use additional words and phrases that are not necessary. Choice *B* is more concise, but uses the present tense of *is*. This does not agree with the rest of the sentence, which uses past tense. The best choice is Choice *D*, which uses the most concise sentence structure and is grammatically correct.

Construction Shift

11. C: The original sentence states that despite the author being nervous, she was able to read with poise and confidence, which is stated in Choice *C*. Choice *A* changes the meaning by adding *because*; however, the author didn't read with confidence *because* she was nervous, but *despite* being nervous. Choice *B* is closer to the original meaning; however, it loses the emphasis of her succeeding *despite* her condition. Choice *D* adds the word *before*, which doesn't make much sense on its own, much less in relation to the original sentence.

12. D: The original sentence states that there was a storm surge and loss of electricity during the hurricane, making Choice *D* correct. Choices *A* and *B* arrange the storm surge and the loss of electricity within a cause and effect statement, which changes the meaning of the original sentence. Choice *C* changes *surge* from a noun into a verb and creates an entirely different situation.

13. B: The original sentence states that an elephant herd will help and support another herd member if it is sick, so Choice *B* is correct. Choice *A* is incorrect because it states the whole herd will be too sick and too tired to walk instead of a single elephant. Choice *C* is incorrect because the original sentence does not say that the herd gathers food when *they* are sick, but when a single member of the herd is sick. Although Choice *D* might be correct in a general sense, it does not relate to the meaning of the original sentence and is therefore incorrect.

14. A: The original sentence says that after a soccer game, they went out to eat. Choice *A* shows the same sequence: they finished the soccer game *then* went out to eat. Choice *B* is incorrect because it reverses the sequence of events. Choices *C* and *D* are incorrect because the words *so* and *because* change the meaning of the original sentence.

15. B: Choice *B* is correct because the idea of the original sentences is Armani getting lost while walking through Paris. Choice *A* is incorrect because it replaces third person with second person. Choice *C* is incorrect because the word *should* indicates an obligation to get lost. Choice *D* is incorrect because it is not specific to the original sentence but instead makes a generalization about getting lost.

16. C: Choice *C* is correct because it shows that Phoenix buried his cat with her favorite toys after she died, which is true of the original statement. Although Choices *A*, *B*, and *D* mention a backyard, the meanings of these choices are skewed. Choice *A* says that Phoenix buried his cat alive, which is incorrect. Choice *B* says his cat died in the backyard, which we do not know to be true. Choice *D* says Phoenix buried his cat after he buried her toys, which is also incorrect.

17. D: Choice *D* is correct because it expresses the sentiment of a moment of joy bringing tears to one's eyes as one sees a sunset while in a helicopter. Choice *A* is incorrect because it implies that the person was outside of the helicopter watching it from afar. Choice *B* is incorrect because the original sentence does not portray the sunset *flying up* into the sky. Choice *C* is incorrect because, while the helicopter may have been facing the sunset, this is not the reason that tears were in the speaker's eyes.

18. B: *B* is correct because like the original sentence, it expresses their plan to go to the party if friends also go. Choice *A* is incorrect because it does not follow the meaning of the original sentence. Choice *C* is incorrect because it states that their friends are going, even though that is not known. Choice *D* is incorrect because it would make the new sentence mean the opposite of the original sentence.

19. C: Choice *C* is correct because the original sentence states that his recovery time was long because his leg was broken before the accident. Choice *A* is incorrect because there is no indication that the man had two broken legs. Choice *B* is incorrect because it indicates that he broke his leg during the car accident, not before. Choice *D* is incorrect because there is no indication that he broke his leg after the car accident.

20. A: Choice *A* is correct because it expresses the fact that the birthday and the party were both after Halloween. Choice *B* is incorrect because it says that the birthday was on Halloween, even though that was not stated in the original sentence. Choice *C* is incorrect because it says the party was specifically a Halloween party and not a birthday party. Choice *D* is incorrect because the party was after Halloween, not before.

Accuplacer English Practice Test #2

Reading Comprehension

Directions for questions 1–10

Read the statement or passage and then choose the best answer to the question. Answer the question based on what is stated or implied in the statement or passage.

1. The Brookside area is an older part of Kansas City, developed mainly in the 1920s and 30s, and is considered one of the nation's first "planned" communities with shops, restaurants, parks, and churches all within a quick walk. A stroll down any street reveals charming two-story Tudor and Colonial homes with smaller bungalows sprinkled throughout the beautiful tree-lined streets. It is common to see lemonade stands on the corners and baseball games in the numerous "pocket" parks tucked neatly behind rows of well-manicured houses. The Brookside shops on 63rd street between Wornall Road and Oak Street are a hub of commerce and entertainment where residents freely shop and dine with their pets (and children) in tow. This is also a common "hangout" spot for younger teenagers because it is easily accessible by bike for most. In short, it is an idyllic neighborhood just minutes from downtown Kansas City.

Which of the following states the main idea of this paragraph?

a. The Brookside shops are a popular hangout for teenagers.
b. There are a number of pocket parks in the Brookside neighborhood.
c. Brookside is a great place to live.
d. Brookside has a high crime rate.

2. At its easternmost part, Long Island opens like the upper and under jaws of some prodigious alligator; the upper and larger one terminating in Montauk Point. The bay that lies in here, and part of which forms the splendid harbor of Greenport, where the Long Island Railroad ends, is called Peconic Bay; and a beautiful and varied water is it, fertile in fish and feathered game. I, who am by no means a skillful fisherman, go down for an hour of a morning on one of the docks, or almost anywhere along shore, and catch a mess of black-fish, which you couldn't buy in New York for a dollar—large fat fellows, with meat on their bones that it takes a pretty long fork to stick through. They have a way here of splitting these fat black-fish and poggies, and broiling them on the coals, beef-steak-fashion, which I recommend your Broadway cooks to copy.

Whitman's comparison of the easternmost part of Long Island to an alligator is an example of which literary device?

a. Hyperbole
b. Simile
c. Personification
d. Alliteration

3. Evidently, our country has overlooked both the importance of learning history and the appreciation of it. But why is this a huge problem? Other than historians, who really cares how the War of 1812 began, or who Alexander the Great's tutor was? Well, not many, as it turns out. So, is history really that important? Yes! History is critical to help us understand the underlying forces that shape decisive events, to prevent us from making the same mistakes twice, and to give us context for current events.

The above is an example of which type of writing?

a. Expository
b. Persuasive
c. Narrative
d. Poetry

4. After applying for a job multiple times, Bob was finally granted an interview. During the interview, he fumbled several questions, mispronounced his potential supervisor's name, and forgot the name of the company. Soon it was clear he knew he wouldn't be working there. At the end of the interview, he stood up and, with *spurious* confidence, shook the interviewer's hand firmly.

Based on the context of the word *spurious*, a good substitution might be:

a. Extreme
b. Mild
c. Fake
d. Genuine

5. Samuel teaches at a high school in one of the biggest cities in the United States. His students come from diverse family backgrounds. Samuel observes that the best students in his class are from homes where parental supervision is minimal. The parents of the bottom five students are the most involved, by a large margin. There are 24 students in his class. Samuel is going to write an academic paper based on his students' family backgrounds and academic performance. The paper will argue that parental involvement is not an important factor in academic success.

Which of the following statements best describes Samuel's sample size?

a. The sample is biased because he has firsthand experience and personal knowledge of its participants.
b. The sample contains too few members to make meaningful claims applicable to a large group.
c. The sample contains too many members to understand the context and specifics of any given student's situation.
d. The sample is unbiased and appropriately sized to draw conclusions on the role of parental supervision in education.

6. Annabelle Rice started having trouble sleeping. Her biological clock was suddenly amiss and she began to lead a nocturnal schedule. She thought her insomnia was due to spending nights writing a horror story, but then she realized that even the idea of going outside into the bright world scared her to bits. She concluded she was now suffering from <u>heliophobia</u>.

Which of the following most accurately describes the meaning of the underlined word in the sentence above?

a. Fear of dreams
b. Fear of sunlight
c. Fear of strangers
d. Anxiety spectrum disorder

7. A famous children's author recently published a historical fiction novel under a pseudonym; however, it did not sell as many copies as her children's books. In her earlier years, she had majored in history and earned a graduate degree in Antebellum American History, which is the time frame of her new novel. Critics praised this newest work far more than the children's series that made her famous. In fact, her

new novel was nominated for the prestigious Albert J. Beveridge Award, but still isn't selling like her children's books, which fly off the shelves because of her name alone.

Which one of the following statements might be accurately inferred based on the above passage?

a. The famous children's author produced an inferior book under her pseudonym.

b. The famous children's author is the foremost expert on Antebellum America.

c. The famous children's author did not receive the bump in publicity for her historical novel that it would have received if it were written under her given name.

d. People generally prefer to read children's series than historical fiction.

8. In 2015, 28 countries, including Estonia, Portugal, Slovenia, and Latvia, scored significantly higher than the United States on standardized high school math tests. In the 1960s, the United States consistently ranked first in the world. Today, the United States spends more than $800 billion dollars on education, which exceeds the next highest country by more than $600 billion dollars. The United States also leads the world in spending per school-aged child by an enormous margin.

If these statements above are factual, which of the following statements must be correct?

a. Outspending other countries on education has benefits beyond standardized math tests.

b. The United States' education system is corrupt and broken.

c. The standardized math tests are not representative of American academic prowess.

d. Spending more money does not guarantee success on standardized math tests.

9. Raul is going to Egypt next month. He has been looking forward to this vacation all year. Since childhood, Raul has been fascinated with pyramids, especially the Great Pyramid of Giza, which is the oldest of the Seven Wonders of the Ancient World. According to religious custom, Egyptian royalty is buried in the tombs located within the pyramid's great labyrinths. Since it has been many years since Raul read about the pyramid's history, he wants to read a book describing how and why the Egyptians built the Great Pyramid thousands of years ago.

Which of the following guides would be the best for Raul?

a. A Beginner's Guide to Giza, a short book describing the city's best historical sites, published by the Egyptian Tourism Bureau (2015)

b. The Life of Zahi Hawass, the autobiography of one of Egypt's most famous archaeologists who was one of the first explorers at Giza (2014)

c. A History of Hieroglyphics, an in-depth look at how archaeologists first broke the ancient code, published by the University of Giza's famed history department (2013)

d. Who Built the Great Pyramids?, a short summary of the latest research and theories on the ancient Egyptians' religious beliefs and archaeological skills, written by a team of leading experts in the field (2015)

10. Last week, we adopted a dog from the local animal shelter, after looking for our perfect pet for several months. We wanted a dog that was not too old, but also past the puppy stage, so that training would be less time-intensive and to give an older animal a home. Robin, as she's called, was a perfect match and we filled out our application and upon approval, were permitted to bring her home. Her physical exam and lab work all confirmed she was healthy. We went to the pet store and bought all sorts of bedding, food, toys, and treats to outfit our house as a dog-friendly and fun place. The shelter told us she liked dry food only, which is a relief because wet food is expensive and pretty off-putting. We even got fencing and installed a dog run in the backyard for Robin to roam unattended. Then we took her to the vet to make sure she was healthy. Next week, she starts the dog obedience class that we enrolled her in with a discount coupon from the shelter. It will be a good opportunity to bond with her and establish commands and dominance. When we took her to the park the afternoon after we adopted her, it was clear that she is a sociable and friendly dog, easily playing cohesively with dogs of all sizes and dispositions.

Which of the following is out of sequence in the story?

a. Last week, we adopted a dog from the local animal shelter, after looking for our perfect pet for several months.
b. Robin, as she's called, was a perfect match and we filled out our application and upon approval, were permitted to bring her home.
c. Her physical exam and lab work all confirmed she was healthy.
d. Next week, she starts the dog obedience class that we enrolled her in with a discount coupon from the shelter.

Directions for questions 11–20

For the questions that follow, two underlined sentences are followed by a question or statement. Read the sentences, then choose the best answer to the question or the best completion of the statement.

11. <u>I'm not going to write about how I conquered the difficult task of actually paying attention in a difficult or unappealing class—it can be done, sure. I have sat through the very epitome of boredom (in my view at least) several times and come away learning something.</u>

What does the second sentence do?

a. It makes a contrast.
b. It restates the information in the first.
c. It provides an example.
d. It disputes the first sentence.

12. <u>If math is being discussed, an instructor can explain the purpose behind the equations or perhaps use real-world applications to show how relevant the topic is. When discussing history, a lecturer can prompt students to imagine themselves in the place of key figures and ask how they might respond.</u>

How are the two sentences related?

a. They provide a cause and effect.
b. They both provide a problem and a solution.
c. They contradict each other.
d. They give examples of the same idea.

13. We know more about dinosaurs than ever before and are still learning fascinating new things about how they looked and lived. However, one has to ask how earlier perceptions continue to influence people's understanding of these creatures?

How are the two sentences related?
  a. They establish a contrast.
  b. They contradict each other.
  c. They present problems and solutions.
  d. They repeat the same idea.

14. The biggest problem with studying dinosaurs is that there are no living dinosaurs to observe. All discoveries associated with these animals are based on physical remains.

What does the second sentence do?
  a. It makes a contrast.
  b. It expands on the first sentence.
  c. It proposes a solution.
  d. It states an effect.

15. Some scientists believe the sail serves to regulate the Spinosaurus' body temperature. Still, other scientists think the sail is used to intimidate other predatory dinosaurs for self-defense.

How are the two sentences related?
  a. They repeat the same idea.
  b. They contradict each other.
  c. They present problems and solutions.
  d. They state a cause and an effect.

16. While it's plausible that dinosaurs share many traits with modern animals, we have been guilty of overattributing these qualities to a unique, extinct species. For much of the early nineteenth century, when people first started studying dinosaur bones, the assumption was that they were simply giant lizards.

What does the second sentence do?
  a. It makes a contrast.
  b. It draws a conclusion.
  c. It reinforces the first.
  d. It states an effect.

17. Usually, all news outlets have some sort of bias, it's just a question of how much bias clouds the reporting. As long as this bias doesn't withhold information from the reader, it can be considered credible.

How are the two sentences related?
  a. They present problems and solutions.
  b. They express roughly the same idea.
  c. They contradict each other.
  d. They establish a contrast.

18. For giving fire (knowledge) to man, Prometheus is punished by the gods, bound to a rock, and tormented for his act. This is clearly a parallel to Frankenstein—he is the modern Prometheus, whose quest for knowledge becomes an obsession.

What does the second sentence do?
  a. It provides a contrast.
  b. It states an effect.
  c. It reinforces the first.
  d. It draws a conclusion.

19. These bigfoot sightings aren't simply a modern occurrence. Ancient civilizations have reported seeing Bigfoot as well.

What does the second sentence do?
  a. It draws a conclusion.
  b. It states an effect.
  c. It reinforces the first.
  d. It provides a contrast.

20. The RV was a great purchase for our family and brought us all closer together. Every morning we would wake up, eat breakfast, and break camp.

What does the second sentence do?
  a. It restates the idea found in the first.
  b. It provides a contrast.
  c. It gives an example.
  d. It presents a contradiction.

Sentence Skills

Sentence Correction

Directions for questions 1–10

Select the best version of the underlined part of the sentence. The first choice is the same as the original sentence. If you think the original sentence is best, choose the first answer.

1. While all dogs descend through gray wolves, it's easy to notice that dog breeds come in a variety of shapes and sizes.
  a. descend through gray wolves
  b. descend by gray wolves
  c. descend from gray wolves
  d. descended through gray wolves

2. With such a drastic range of traits, appearances and body types dogs are one of the most variable and adaptable species on the planet.
  a. drastic range of traits, appearances and body types
  b. drastic range of traits, appearances, and body types
  c. drastic range of traits and appearances and body types
  d. drastic range of traits, appearances, as well as body types

3. Since the first discovery of dinosaur bones, scientists has made strides in technological development and methodologies used to investigate these extinct animals.

a. scientists has made strides in technological development and methodologies used to investigate
b. scientists has made strides in technological development, and methodologies, used to investigate
c. scientists have made strides in technological development and methodologies used to investigate
d. scientists, have made strides in technological development and methodologies used, to investigate

4. Paleontologists know this sail exists and have ideas for the function of the sail however they are uncertain of which idea is the true function.

a. the sail however they are uncertain of which idea is the true function.
b. the sail however, they are uncertain of which idea is the true function.
c. the sail however they are, uncertain, of which idea is the true function.
d. the sail; however, they are uncertain of which idea is the true function.

5. Usually, all news outlets have some sort of bias, it's just a question of how much bias clouds the reporting.

a. outlets have some sort of bias, it's just a question of how much
b. outlets have some sort of bias. Just a question of how much
c. outlets have some sort of bias it can just be a question of how much
d. outlets have some sort of bias, its just a question of how much

6. Besides the novel's engaging writing style the story's central theme remains highly relevant in a world of constant discovery and moral dilemmas.

a. writing style the story's central theme
b. writing style the central theme of the story
c. writing style, the story's central theme
d. the story's central theme's writing style

7. Looking deeper into the myth of Prometheus sheds light not only on the character of Frankenstein but also poses a psychological dilemma to the audience.

a. but also poses a psychological dilemma to the audience
b. but also poses a psychological dilemma with the audience
c. but also poses a psychological dilemma for the audience
d. but also poses a psychological dilemma there before the audience

8. There are many things to consider when addressing this question but the chief factor is whether there is credible evidence.

a. this question but the chief factor
b. this question, but the chief factor
c. this question however the chief factor
d. this question; but the chief factor

9. For science to formally recognize that such a species exists, there needs to be physical proof.

a. For science to formally recognize that such a species exists, there needs to be physical proof.
b. Physical proof are needed in order for science to formally recognize that such a species exists.
c. For science to formally recognize that such a species exists there needs to be physical proof.
d. For science, to formally recognize that such a species exists, there needs to be physical proof.

10. Today, laws prohibit the <u>use of unnecessary force in self-defense; these serve to eliminate</u> beating someone to a pulp once they have been neutralized.

a. use of unnecessary force in self-defense; these serve to eliminate
b. use of unnecessary force in self-defense serving to eliminate
c. use of unnecessary force, in self-defense, these serve to eliminate
d. use of unnecessary force. In self-defense, these serve to eliminate

Construction Shift

Directions for questions 11–20

Rewrite the sentence in your head following the directions given below. Keep in mind that your new sentence should be well written and should have essentially the same meaning as the original sentence.

11. Over time, certain traits develop in animals that enable them to thrive in these environments.

Rewrite, beginning with

<u>Animals thrive in these environments</u>

The next words will be

a. over a certain amount of time with changing traits.
b. which contain traits that allow animals to thrive.
c. and animals have changing traits over time.
d. due to certain traits in them that develop over time.

12. I've sat through many lectures and always come away learning something.

Rewrite, beginning with

<u>I have always learned something</u>

The next words will be

a. from the many lectures I've sat through.
b. when I sit through lectures.
c. and have sat through many lectures.
d. from going away to many lectures.

13. After we went rollerblading, we decided to eat a pretzel, but not before we washed our hands.

Rewrite, beginning with

<u>We ate a pretzel</u>

The next words will be

a. before we went rollerblading and after we washed our hands.
b. after we went rollerblading and washed our hands.
c. before we washed our hands and after we went rollerblading.
d. before we washed our hands and went rollerblading.

14. I used to like the movie *Star Gazing* more than the movie *Comet*, but as time goes by, I find that *Comet* is the better of the two.

Rewrite, beginning with

<u>Now that some time has passed,</u>

The next words will be

a. I believe the movie *Star Gazing* is better than the movie *Comet*, although I used to think *Comet* was a much better movie between the two.
b. the movies *Comet* and *Star Gazing* are both much better than I remember them, with the movie *Comet* being the more preferred movie among its audience.
c. I no longer like the movie *Star Gazing*, but the movie *Comet* has become my new favorite because it is the better movie of the two.
d. I see that between the movies *Comet* and *Star Gazing*, *Comet* is the better movie, although I used to like *Star Gazing* more.

15. I drank the lemonade because I ate the sugar cookies and needed something to wash them down.

Rewrite, beginning with

<u>I ate the sugar cookies</u>

The next words will be

a. but not before I washed them down with lemonade.
b. although I needed to wash them down with lemonade.
c. and then needed to wash them down with lemonade.
d. and they were washed down, so I drank the lemonade.

16. If she had enough money, she would have her wedding at the country club.

Rewrite, beginning with

<u>She cannot have her wedding at the country club</u>

The next words will be

a. because she has enough money.
b. although she lacks the money.
c. since she lacks the money.
d. if she had enough money.

17. I cannot go to the movies unless I first take out the trash.

Rewrite, beginning with

I took out the trash;

The next words will be

a. meanwhile, I can go to the movies.
b. therefore, I can go to the movies.
c. so I cannot go to the movies.
d. owing to the fact that I went to the movies.

18. We were all devastated when Melissa told us she was moving to Canada.

Rewrite, beginning with

Melissa said she was moving to Canada,

The next words will be

a. this devastated us.
b. because we were all devastated.
c. and we were devastated.
d. which we were devastated by.

19. Jordan was so happy to see his sister that he threw confetti into the air.

Rewrite, beginning with

Feeling happy to see his sister,

The next words will be

a. Jordan threw confetti in the air.
b. confetti was thrown into the air.
c. when Jordan threw confetti in the air.
d. he threw confetti into the air.

20. The inventory check was almost over when Harry brought everyone donuts.

Rewrite, beginning with

Harry brought everyone donuts

The next words will be

a. after the inventory check was over.
b. because the inventory check was over.
c. the inventory check was almost over.
d. before the inventory check was over.

Practice Prompt

Prepare an essay of about 300–600 words on the topic below.

> Coaches of kids' sports teams are increasingly concerned about the behavior of parents at games. Parents are screaming and cursing at coaches, officials, players, and other parents. Physical fights have even broken out at games. Parents need to be reminded that coaches are volunteers, giving up their time and energy to help kids develop in their chosen sport. The goal of kids' sports teams is to learn and develop skills, but it's also to have fun. When parents are out of control at games and practices, it takes the fun out of the sport.

Take a side on the issue. Use specific examples to support your argument.

Answer Explanations #2

Reading Comprehension

1. C: All the details in this paragraph suggest that Brookside is a great place to live, plus the last sentence states that it is an *idyllic neighborhood*, meaning it is perfect, happy, and blissful. Choices *A* and *B* are incorrect, because although they do contain specific details from the paragraph that support the main idea, they are not the main idea. Choice *D* is incorrect because there is no reference in the paragraph to the crime rate in Brookside.

2. B: Choice *B* is correct because a *simile* is a comparison between two unlike things using the words *like* or *as*. Choice *A* is incorrect because *hyperbole* is an exaggeration for affect. Choice *C* is incorrect because *personification* attributes human characteristics to an inanimate object. Choice *D* is incorrect because *alliteration* is a poetic device in which several words begin with the same letter or letters. It is used to add emphasis or affect.

3. B: Persuasive is the correct answer because the author is clearly trying to convey the point that history education is very important. Choice *A* is incorrect because expository writing is more informational and less emotional. Choice *C* is incorrect because narrative writing involves story telling. Choice *D* is incorrect because this is a piece of prose, not poetry.

4. C: To arrive at the correct answer, find the best synonym for *spurious*. *Fake* makes the most sense because Bob is trying to hide his true emotions. Based on his horrible performance, he understands that he didn't get the job, so the reader can infer that his confidence is not at an all-time high. Therefore, *fake* would make just as much sense in this case as *spurious*. *Extreme* would indicate that Bob is euphoric and the interview went well. *Mild* would indicate that Bob thought he had a slight chance at getting hired. In this instance, *genuine* would be an antonym; i.e., the exact opposite of what Bob is feeling.

5. B: Samuel wants to write an academic paper based on his 24 students. His best students come from homes where parental supervision is minimal, while the worst come from parents with extensive involvement. His conclusion is counterintuitive and probably the result of a small sample size. Choices A and D having to do with bias, is not the issue, nor is Choice *C*. Samuel's experience with these students is not applicable to students in general; rather, it is a tiny sample size relative to the millions of school children in the United States. The correct answer is B since the sample contains too few members to make meaningful claims applicable to a large group.

6. B: The passage indicates that Annabelle has a fear of going outside into the daylight. Thus *heliophobia* must refer to a fear of bright lights or sunlight. Choice *B* is the only answer that describes this.

7. C: We are looking for an inference—a conclusion that is reached on the basis of evidence and reasoning—from the passage that will likely explain why the famous children's author did not achieve her usual success with the new genre (despite the book's acclaim). Choice *A* is wrong because the statement is false according to the passage. Choice *B* is wrong because, although the passage says the author has a graduate degree on the subject, it would be an unrealistic leap to infer that she is the foremost expert on Antebellum America. Choice *D* is wrong because there is nothing in the passage to lead us to infer that people generally prefer a children's series to historical fiction. In contrast, Choice *C* can be logically inferred since the passage speaks of the great success of the children's series and the declaration that the fame of the author's name causes the children's books to "fly off the shelves." Thus, she did not receive any bump from her name since she published the historical novel under a pseudonym, and Choice *C* is correct.

8. D: Outspending other countries on education could have other benefits, but there is no reference to this in the passage, so Choice *A* is incorrect. Choice *B* is incorrect because the author does not mention corruption. Choice *C* is incorrect because there is nothing in the passage stating that the tests are not genuinely representative. Choice *D* is accurate because spending more money has not brought success. The United States already spends the most money, and the country is not excelling on these tests. Choice *D* is the correct answer.

9. D: Raul wants a book that describes how and why ancient Egyptians built the Great Pyramid of Giza. Choice *A* is incorrect because it focuses more generally on Giza as a whole, rather than the Great Pyramid itself. Choice *B* is close but incorrect because it is an autobiography that will largely focus on the archaeologist's life. Choice *C* is wrong because it focuses on hieroglyphics; it is not directly on point. Choice *D*, the book directly covering the building of the Great Pyramids, should be most helpful.

10. C: The passage is told in chronological order, detailing the steps the family took to adopt their dog. The narrator mentions that Robin's physical exam and lab work confirmed she was healthy before discussing that they brought her to the vet to evaluate her health. It is illogical that lab work would confirm good health prior to an appointment with the vet, when presumably, the lab work would be collected.

11. C: The second sentence provides an example of the first. The first sentence states that the task of paying attention can be done, and the second sentence explains *how* this can be done by a personal example. There is no contrast in the second sentence, making Choice *A* incorrect. The information is an example, not a restatement, making Choice *B* incorrect. Choice *D* is incorrect; there is no dispute in the second sentence.

12. D: They give examples of the same idea. The idea behind both sentences is that an instructor can explore a lecture in a concrete way rather than simply state facts or statistics. The two sentences do not represent cause and effect, making Choice *A* incorrect. There is no specific problem stated in either sentence, making Choice *B* incorrect. They do not contradict each other—if anything, they reinforce each other, making Choice *C* incorrect.

13. A: They establish a contrast. The word "however" is always indicative of a contrast in a passage. The first sentence contemplates the many things we know about dinosaurs, the second sentence is the beginning of a contrast stating that our perceptions are coming from earlier influences. They do not contradict each other, so Choice *B* is incorrect. There is no problem or solution in either sentence, but rather a question, so Choice *C* is incorrect. They do not repeat the same idea, but provide a contrast, so Choice *D* is incorrect.

14. B: The second sentence expands on the first sentence. The first sentence states how it's hard to study dinosaurs because they are not living, and the second sentence expands on that by saying indeed, the discoveries are based on physical remains (rather than a living, breathing thing). Choice *A* is incorrect, as the second sentence does not make a contrast in any way, but rather agrees with the first. Choice *C* is incorrect; there is no solution here. Choice *D* is incorrect; the second sentence would not be considered an effect of the first because they are talking about the same idea: how we go about observing dinosaurs.

15. B: The two sentences contradict each other. Some scientists believe A, and some scientists believe B, and these two ideas contradict each other in reality. The two ideas about the purpose of the sail do not repeat each other, so Choice *A* is incorrect. There is no problem and solution depicted, and there is no cause and effect depicted, so Choices *C* and *D* are incorrect.

16. C: To reinforce something means to support with additional material. We are given information in the first sentence about mistaking the qualities of dinosaurs, and in the second sentence this idea is reinforced by the admission that scientists thought dinosaurs were simply giant lizards. Choice *A* is incorrect; there is no contrast in the second sentence. Choice *B* is incorrect; the second sentence doesn't draw a conclusion, but rather offers information to reinforce the first sentence. Choice *D* is incorrect; there is no cause and effect relationship between the two sentences.

17. A: The first sentence depicts a problem: bias in news outlets. The second sentence provides a solution: the act of not withholding information from the reader and the assertion of credibility. This is the best answer choice among the others. The sentences are not repetitive of each other, so Choice *B* is incorrect. They do not contradict each other or establish a contrast, so Choices *C* and *D* are incorrect.

18. D: The second sentence draws a conclusion from the first. To draw a conclusion means to take information that is presented and infer meaning to it. The first sentence gives us information; the myth of Prometheus and what happened to him. The second sentence makes a parallel between Frankenstein and Prometheus, and thereby draws a conclusion that they are similar due to this myth. The other answer choices are incorrect.

19. C: The second sentence reinforces the first by giving additional material to prove that bigfoot sightings aren't simply a modern occurrence. Choice *A* is incorrect; the sentence is better described as reinforcing the first with extra material rather than drawing a conclusion. Choice *B* is incorrect; there is no cause or effect relationship here. Choice *D* is also incorrect, as there is no contrast between the two sentences.

20. C: The second sentence provides an example of how purchasing the RV brought the family closer: a new morning routine spent together. Choice *A* is incorrect because the information in the two sentences is not repetitive or has not been restated. Choice *B* and *D* are incorrect; there is no contrast or contradiction between the two sentences.

Sentence Skills

Sentence Correction

1. C: Choice *C* correctly uses *from* to describe the fact that dogs are related to wolves. The word *through* is incorrectly used here, so Choices *A* is incorrect. Choice *B* makes no sense. Choice *D* unnecessarily changes the verb tense in addition to incorrectly using *through*.

2. B: Choice *B* is correct because the Oxford comma is applied, clearly separating the specific terms. Choice *A* lacks this clarity. Choice *C* is correct but too wordy since commas can be easily applied. Choice *D* doesn't flow with the sentence's structure.

3. C: Choice *C* is correct because it fixes the core issue with this sentence: the singular *has* should not describe the plural *scientists*. Thus, Choice *A* is incorrect. Choices *B* and *D* add unnecessary commas.

4. D: Choice *D* correctly applies a semicolon to introduce a new line of thought while remaining in a single sentence. The comma after *however* is also appropriately placed. Choice *A* is a run-on sentence. Choice *B* is also incorrect because the single comma is not enough to fix the sentence. Choice *C* adds commas around *uncertain* which are unnecessary.

5. A: Choice *A* is correct because the sentence contains no errors. The comma after *bias* successfully links the two halves of the sentence, and the use of *it's* is correct as a contraction of *it is*. Choice *B* creates a sentence fragment, while Choice *C* creates a run-on. Choice *D* incorrectly changes *it's* to *its*.

6. C: Choice *C* correctly adds a comma after *style*, successfully joining the dependent and the independent clause as a single sentence. Choice *A* is incorrect because the dependent and independent clauses remain unsuccessfully combined without the comma. Choices *B* and *D* do nothing to fix this.

7. A: Choice *A* is correct, as *not only* and *but also* are correlative pairs. In this sentence, *but* successfully transitions the first part into the second half, making punctuation unnecessary. Additionally, the use of *to* indicates that an idea or challenge is being presented to the reader. Choice *B*'s *with*, *C*'s *for*, and *D*'s *there before* are not as active, meaning these revisions weaken the sentence.

8. B: Choice *B* correctly joins the two independent clauses with a comma before *but*. Choice *A* is incorrect because, without the comma, it is a run-on sentence. Choice *C* also lacks punctuation and uses *however*, which should be reserved for starting a new sentence or perhaps after a semicolon. Choice *D* is incorrect because the semicolon throws off the sentence structure and is incorrectly used; the correct revision would have also removed *but*.

9. A: Choice *A* is correct because the sentence does not require modification. Choice *B* is incorrect because it uses the faulty subject/verb agreement, "Physical proof are." Choice *C* is incorrect because a comma would need to follow *exists*. Choice *D* is incorrect because the comma after *science* is unnecessary.

10. A: Choice *A* is the best answer for several reasons. To begin, the section is grammatically correct in using a semicolon to connect the two independent clauses. This allows the different two ideas to be connected without separating them. In this context, the semicolon makes more sense for the overall sentence structure and passage as a whole. Choice *B* is incorrect because it forms a run-on. Choice *C* applies a comma in incorrect positions. Choice *D* separates the sentence in a place that does not make sense for the context.

Construction Shift

11. D: The best answer is Choice *D* because it keeps the original meaning of the sentence with the transitional phrase *due to*. Choice *A* is incorrect; the sentence says that the animals thrive *with* these changing traits over time, but it does not say the animals thrive *because of* these traits. Choice *B* is incorrect because the sentence suggests it is the *environments* and not the *animals* that contain the traits. Choice *C* is incorrect; it says that animals thrive and that they have changing traits that develop, but it fails to show a connection between the two.

12. A: Choice *A* is correct because the meaning is the closest in similarity to the original; there is learning that occurs from the past lectures the speaker has sat through. Choice *B* is incorrect because it changes the tense of the act of sitting through lectures. Choice *C* is incorrect because it uses the conjunction *and* which fails to connect the two clauses. Choice *D* is incorrect because although it uses similar language, it changes the meaning to say that the speaker *goes away* to lectures.

13. B: The best answer is "We ate a pretzel after we went rollerblading and washed our hands." Choice *A* says we ate a pretzel before we went rollerblading, which is incorrect. Choice *C* says we ate a pretzel before we washed our hands, which is incorrect. Choice *D* says we ate a pretzel before we washed our hands and went rollerblading, which is the opposite of the original meaning.

14. D: Choice *D* is the best answer because it is closest to the original sentence. Choice *A* is incorrect because it says the opposite movie is preferred than the original sentence. Choice *B* is incorrect; although it keeps with *Comet* being the more preferred movie, it makes some additions about audience that are not in the original sentence. Choice *C* is incorrect; the original sentence does not say it doesn't like *Star Gazing*; it only says that *Comet* is the better of the two.

15. C: Choice *C* is the best answer choice because it gives the appropriate cause and effect relationship: I ate the cookies and then drank the lemonade. Choice *A* is incorrect because the order is swapped. Choice *B* is incorrect because it introduces the word "although," which implies the choice to drink lemonade was made *in spite* of eating the cookies rather than *because of* eating the cookies. Choice *D* is incorrect because it changes the meaning; the cookies were not "washed down," but the lemonade was used to wash the cookies down.

16. C: Choice *C* is the best answer choice. The sentence implies that with enough money, she would have her wedding at the country club. The new sentence states that she cannot have her wedding there, and we can infer this is because she lacks the money. Choice *A* is incorrect; she does not have enough money from the rewrite. Choice *B* is incorrect; the word *although* means *despite*, and this does not follow logically from the original sentence. Choice *D* is incorrect; if she had enough money, she *could* have her wedding at the country club, but the rewrite says she *cannot*.

17. B: Choice *B* is the correct answer. The original sentence says the speaker can go to the movies if they take out the trash, and Choice *B* expresses this same sentiment. Choice *A* is incorrect because the word *meanwhile* implies *at the same time*, and the original sentence says the trash must be taken out first. Choice *C* is incorrect because it contradicts the original truth of the sentence. Choice *D* is incorrect because it switches the order of the movies and taking out the trash.

18. C: Choice *C* is the best answer because it has no grammatical errors and retains the original sentence meaning. Choice *A* is incorrect because it creates a comma splice. Choice *B* is incorrect because it changes the meaning of the sentence; Melissa didn't move because we were devastated—we were devastated because Melissa moved. Choice *D* is incorrect because it doesn't use the best wording by ending with "by." Choice *C* is much more straightforward in its meaning.

19. A: Choice *A* is the best answer choice because we are given the subject, "Jordan," and verb, "threw" in a straightforward sentence that retains the meaning of the original sentence. Choice *B* is incorrect because the sentence is passive and there is no subject to tell who threw the confetti. Choice *C* is incorrect; both sides of the comma are dependent clauses, and dependent clauses cannot stand in a sentence without an independent clause. Choice *D* is incorrect; the pronoun "he" should be replaced by the noun, "Jordan," since we are not given that information in the rewrite.

20. D: Choice *D* is the best answer. We see in the original sentence that the inventory was *almost* over, but not over yet, when Harry brought donuts. Therefore, he must have brought them *before* the inventory check was over. Choice *A* is incorrect because it says Harry brought them *after* the check was over. Choice *B* is incorrect because, again, the inventory check is not over yet when Harry brings the donuts. Choice *C* is incorrect because this creates a run-on sentence. We need a semicolon or a conjunction to separate the two independent clauses.

Dear ACCUPLACER Test Taker,

We would like to start by thanking you for purchasing this study guide for your ACCUPLACER exam. We hope that we exceeded your expectations.

Our goal in creating this study guide was to cover all of the topics that you will see on the test. We also strove to make our practice questions as similar as possible to what you will encounter on test day. With that being said, if you found something that you feel was not up to your standards, please send us an email and let us know.

We would also like to let you know about other books in our catalog that may interest you.

ACCUPLACER

This can be found on Amazon: amazon.com/dp/162845492X

Next-Generation ACCUPLACER

amazon.com/dp/1628454253

TSI

amazon.com/dp/162845511X

SAT Math 1

amazon.com/dp/1628454717

AP Biology

amazon.com/dp/1628454989

We have study guides in a wide variety of fields. If the one you are looking for isn't listed above, then try searching for it on Amazon or send us an email.

Thanks Again and Happy Testing!
Product Development Team
info@studyguideteam.com

Interested in buying more than 10 copies of our product? Contact us about bulk discounts:

bulkorders@studyguideteam.com

FREE Test Taking Tips DVD Offer

To help us better serve you, we have developed a Test Taking Tips DVD that we would like to give you for FREE. **This DVD covers world-class test taking tips that you can use to be even more successful when you are taking your test.**

All that we ask is that you email us your feedback about your study guide. Please let us know what you thought about it – whether that is good, bad or indifferent.

To get your **FREE Test Taking Tips DVD**, email freedvd@studyguideteam.com with "FREE DVD" in the subject line and the following information in the body of the email:

a. The title of your study guide.

b. Your product rating on a scale of 1-5, with 5 being the highest rating.

c. Your feedback about the study guide. What did you think of it?

d. Your full name and shipping address to send your free DVD.

If you have any questions or concerns, please don't hesitate to contact us at freedvd@studyguideteam.com.

Thanks again!

55842356R00052

Made in the USA
Columbia, SC
18 April 2019